IMAGES
of America

ROCKVILLE

This painting by local artist Houston Hancock shows the center of Rockville in the mid-1950s. Two courthouses on the right visually define it as the seat of Montgomery County, Maryland. Beyond are the small-scale business buildings that made up its commercial core—most of which would be demolished in about a decade for a massive urban renewal project that triggered repercussions felt for decades. (Courtesy of Houston Hancock.)

On the Cover: This 1954 view of the heart of Rockville looks toward the main intersection of Montgomery Avenue and Washington Street. The junction of early thoroughfares spawned a colonial community that would not only become the seat of Maryland's largest county but also a major suburb of the nation's capital that is now one of the most ethnically diverse cities in the nation. (Courtesy of Peerless Rockville Historic Preservation, Ltd.)

IMAGES
of America

ROCKVILLE

Peerless Rockville Historic Preservation, Ltd.,
with Ralph Buglass

ARCADIA
PUBLISHING

Published by Arcadia Publishing
Charleston, South Carolina

Printed in the United States of America

Library of Congress Control Number: 2019953709

For all general information, please contact Arcadia Publishing:
Telephone 843-853-2070
Fax 843-853-0044
E-mail sales@arcadiapublishing.com
For customer service and orders:
Toll-Free 1-888-313-2665

Visit us on the Internet at www.arcadiapublishing.com

This book is dedicated to the many "peerless" volunteers, contributors, and supporters for remembering and guarding our shared Rockville heritage.

CONTENTS

ACKNOWLEDGMENTS

Rockville, Maryland, shines in this volume through the many rare images—culled by researchers, donors, and volunteers over 40 years—and the thoroughly researched and charming writing of Ralph Buglass; he has marvelously pieced together a visual overview of Rockville over time. I cannot overstate my appreciation to him and to all our many valued volunteers and supporters for all they contribute in other ways.

On behalf of the board and members of Peerless Rockville Historic Preservation, I am delighted to present this pictorial account of Rockville's history. Please enjoy this nostalgic dive into Rockville's past, allow yourself to linger over the photographs, as we often do, and settle in to learn more about the history that surrounds you.

Peerless Rockville has the distinction of serving as stewards of Rockville's built heritage and keepers of its history—but in this, we do not act alone. Through collaborations with local partner organizations, professional and volunteer historians, researchers, designers, archivists, and with the support of the City of Rockville, we work to protect and share the memories of the people, places, and happenings, both large and small, that have culminated to create Rockville's unique identity.

Almost any presentation of Rockville's history—certainly this pictorial account—owes a foundational debt of gratitude to our historians, be they volunteers, professionals, founders, or board or staff members, and especially to the work of Eileen S. McGuckian, who, at various times, has acted as all of the above while tirelessly documenting and safeguarding Rockville history for decades. From the earliest days of Peerless Rockville's founding, when much of "old" Rockville had fallen victim to a wholesale modern makeover, Eileen has acted as a force for preservation of a quite remarkable "peerless" city's heritage. Also the author of the elegantly written *Rockville: Portrait of a City*—the definitive history of our city, on which this volume draws heavily—she is a cherished mentor and role model for those of us carrying on the work—while still trying to keep up with her.

Most of the photographs in this volume come from Peerless Rockville's extensive archives; we wish to acknowledge in particular the collection of professional photographer Roy Perry and the photographs of Lewis Reed, Malcolm Walter, and Dean Evangelista, whose priceless images captured over different time periods have been generously donated to us; equal recognition goes to Charles Brewer, whose collection of images acquired from numerous sources is also a key part of the Peerless archives.

Additionally, we have drawn greatly on the photographic collection of Montgomery History, our county's historical society and a partner in many ways. Archivist and librarian Sarah Hedlund was unfailingly helpful and astoundingly prompt. Other sources—both institutional and individuals—to whom we are equally grateful are credited at the end of captions accompanying their images. Photographs without parenthetical attribution are from Peerless Rockville's archive; those taken especially for this volume by Ralph Buglass are indicated by his initials, RB.

—Nancy Pickard, Executive Director
Peerless Rockville Historic Preservation, Ltd.

INTRODUCTION

So we beat on, boats against the current, borne back ceaselessly into the past.
—The Great Gatsby, F. Scott Fitzgerald

This last line of *The Great Gatsby* aptly sets the stage for this look into Rockville's past—not simply because the author F. Scott Fitzgerald is buried here. Rockville's evolution into the robust, diverse city it is today is the result of the endless currents of time, with ebbs and flows, highs and lows, progress and loss—change ever occurring.

This pictorial history seeks to cover the wide sweep of Rockville's transformation over time through precious visual reminders of its various incarnations and different stages in its history.

Touted as a "peerless" place to live when developing as a suburb of the nation's capital in the late 1800s with the arrival of train service, Rockville is a distinctive city in its own right, winning an All-America City award four times and frequently cited as a "best place to live." A tiny colonial-era crossroads when picked to be the seat of the surrounding county, two centuries later it was Maryland's second-largest city, having boomed after World War II.

As it grew, Rockville became a collection of distinctive neighborhoods whose residents now represent so many ethnicities that it is among the nation's most demographically diverse cities. Still one of the state's 10 most populous cities, it is perhaps best known not simply as a county seat, but the government home for what has become one of the nation's wealthiest counties that people from the world over now call home. For others, it is associated primarily with the eponymous Rockville Pike, a bustling commercial strip that was not even paved until 1925—itself a reflection of the sweeping changes Rockville has experienced.

Rockville's history is notable in other regards. It has figured in important national events—the Civil War, for one. As in much of Maryland—a southern state that did not secede—Rockville residents were divided in their allegiances, though loyalties were not always clear-cut. Staunch Southern sympathizers, slave owners who opposed secession, and ardent Unionists all could be found in Rockville—sometimes within families and churches. Union soldiers camped just outside town for much of the war; troops from both sides often passed through, even engaging in several skirmishes right in town.

Perhaps of greatest consequence, Confederate general J.E.B. Stuart's forces were delayed in getting to the crucial battle at Gettysburg after spending most of a day in Rockville rounding up Unionists and supplies—not to mention flirting with adoring attendees of a local girls' school. Whether that delay contributed to the Confederate defeat—a turning point in the war—is tantalizing conjecture.

Roughly a century after the Civil War, the civil rights struggle, nearly as contentious, took on national importance; Rockville figured significantly in this issue, too. An early civil rights milestone occurred in Rockville with a groundbreaking legal victory by Thurgood Marshall in a school segregation case 17 years before his landmark *Brown v. Board of Education* US Supreme Court victory declaring "separate but equal" inherently unequal.

Education on a more local level played a big part in Rockville's history as well. An early state-chartered private academy, Montgomery County's first public high school, and the only black high school for the entire county were all located here.

The city also has had ties to other important figures besides the famous *Great Gatsby* author and Marshall, the first African American Supreme Court justice. Josiah Henson was once enslaved on a plantation just outside Rockville; his autobiography, published after he escaped to Canada with the intent of raising money to free his brother still enslaved in Rockville, was the inspiration for Harriet Beecher Stowe's enormously influential antislavery novel *Uncle Tom's Cabin*.

Through most of the 20th century, Rockville was home to a preeminent private psychiatric facility that was the basis for another novel, *I Never Promised You a Rose Garden*, and the facility's renowned therapist, Dr. Frieda Fromm-Reichmann, was the model for the beloved Dr. Fried in the novel.

"Peerless" indeed—even from colonial times when Rockville was known only by the name of a tavern located here. In 1774, the Hungerford Resolves, a proclamation by a group of influential men adopted in the tavern and named for it, voiced risky revolutionary sentiments, calling for an end to trade with England as "the most effectual means for the securing of American Freedom" in the wake of the Boston Tea Party.

An even earlier tavern had given the tiny crossroads its first name—Owen's Ordinary (so it might be said Rockville was once merely "ordinary"). When Montgomery County, named for the first general killed in the American Revolution, was carved out of southern Frederick County in 1776, the centrally located community was selected as the county seat and was then known as Montgomery Court House. For a time, it was also called Williamsburgh for early landowners. But eventually, Rockville—likely derived from nearby Rock Creek—became its permanent name.

Over time, of course, Rockville gained an ever-increasing variety of businesses, churches, schools, a library, and other elements that typically make up the fabric of a community, and as is customary, neighborhoods evolved—in Rockville's case, each quite different from another in character, based largely on home styles and when they developed. Yet, there were quite out-of-the-ordinary community features as well.

Rockville once had a racetrack, boasted an airport, and took a chance on buying a mansion now open to the public as an event center, later adding a theater to the site. One resident's backyard telescope presaged an international observatory built nearby. The airport site became a shopping center in the 1950s, and the pike on which it fronted boomed.

In contrast, the city's downtown—a mix of structures built over the span of decades, each characteristic of its time and even having a certain charm as a result—was deteriorating. So Rockville embarked on a major urban renewal project to create a "new Rockville." It was as much a turning point in Rockville's history as anything before or since.

Much of Rockville's main street was razed, replaced by an enclosed shopping mall and residential complex. The results were decidedly mixed. The mall, an imposing concrete structure, struggled to attract either stores or shoppers and was gone in just over 20 years. The housing development—ahead of its time with a mix of townhomes clustered about high-rise and garden-style apartment buildings—still anchors one end of Rockville's downtown. But a downtown that today might be viewed as historic was lost—lamentably so, to many.

All this and more make up Rockville's history—visually told on the following pages through vintage photographs so that readers can see for themselves what once was and what has been preserved. Memories, it is said, are priceless; Rockville's heritage, it may be said, is rich and perhaps priceless, even in some respects peerless—definitely not ordinary!

One

ROCKVILLE AT A CROSSROADS

In 1755, British soldiers led by Gen. Edward Braddock, on their way to fight in the French and Indian War preceding the American Revolution, camped at a sparsely settled spot where two crude roads—previously nomadic Native American trails—met. There was little more than a tavern on one corner. A soldier recorded in his journal that the location was called "Owings Oardianary," named for the ordinary, or tavern, owned by a man named Lawrence Owens. The soldier noted the spot was "very dirty."

The soldier's account is the earliest written documentation of the location that would have other names before becoming Rockville but, more importantly, given its central crossroads location, be designated the seat of a new Maryland county created the same year the colonies declared independence from Britain—for which local patriots had declared early support while meeting in a later tavern.

One of those early roads would become important as a main thoroughfare—once called the Great Road, later a toll road, and now the Rockville Pike. In one direction, it led to the newly designated capital of the young nation—just 15 miles to the south—and the existing Potomac River port of George Town; the other way went to Maryland's second-largest city, Frederick Town, and the promising frontier beyond it. As the county seat and because of its location along this important roadway, Rockville's growth was assured, but long in coming.

This opening chapter looks at the community's early evolution from its colonial roots through the Civil War. As the small village grew, Rockville's remarkable story began unfolding.

A stone marker next to the Red Brick Courthouse, itself a historic icon, commemorates the expedition of British general Edward Braddock in 1755 through what Rockville was then known as—Owens Ordinary, for a tavern at the crossroads. The journal of one of Braddock's soldiers provides the earliest description of the tiny colonial village. (RB photograph.)

The village later became known as Hungerford's Tavern for this establishment run by Charles Hungerford. It catered to travelers and served as a local meeting place, as when the Hungerford Resolves were adopted in 1774. The first court sessions were held here after Montgomery County was created in 1776. Shown on a 1906 postcard, it stood until 1913.

This 1811 painting, "Out of Robb's Window, Montgomery Court House" (as the town was also known for a time after becoming the county seat), is one of its earliest depictions. The artist was Benjamin Latrobe, architect of the US Capitol, who was staying at Adam Robb's tavern with his ailing son in hopes the country air would prove beneficial. (Courtesy of Montgomery History.)

This 1803 "Plan of Rockville" is its earliest map. Adam Robb's tavern was in section I (lower right); the exact location is unknown. Hungerford's Tavern was nearby at Jefferson and Washington Streets on No. 19. The notch on the right was a portion of what is now Courthouse Square; it is believed the first actual courthouse, a simple wood-frame structure, was built there about 1788.

By 1840, Montgomery County government operated out of this brick building in Courthouse Square. It and a nearby jail constituted county government. Lawyers opened offices close to the courthouse, joining a growing, but still modest, number of merchants in the town. The population numbered fewer than 300.

This is the oldest-known photograph of Rockville, dated to between the mid-1860s and early 1870s. It shows Courthouse Square and the main road leading to Washington—one of the crossroads that was the town's reason for being. On the left is a hay scale, a reminder of the numerous farms just beyond the town's boundaries. On the other side behind the iron fence stood the courthouse shown in the previous photograph.

One of the earliest, and grandest, houses was built in 1815 by Upton Beall, who lived in Georgetown when he succeeded his father as second clerk of the court; required to move to Rockville, he wanted a house as elegant as many in Georgetown. This photograph is from 1973 when the structure was listed in the National Register of Historic Places; it is now the house museum of the county's historical society, Montgomery History.

Most other homes were far more modest, such as this one—surviving today but in altered form—at 101 North Adams Street. Once Adam Robb's home, this is how it looked about 1900 when it faced Middle Lane. Just a half block away is 5 North Adams Street, a portion of which was built in 1793, making it the oldest extant house in Rockville. With the Beall-Dawson House right across the street, they made up Rockville's oldest residential neighborhood.

An early Rockville hotel, the Montgomery House, opposite the courthouse, was patronized by travelers and county residents having business in town, which was not a one-day trip for many. During the Civil War, it was used by Union and Confederate commanders—at different times of course—reflecting how Rockville was on occasion caught up in the war.

Dr. Edward Stonestreet practiced medicine out of this small office next to his house from 1853 until his 1903 death. One of two pre–Civil War Rockville physicians, he performed induction examinations and surgery for the Army during the war and had charge of a temporary military hospital on the courthouse grounds. This cherished building later served as the town's library and is now a museum of 19th-century medicine on the grounds of Montgomery History.

Montgomery Sentinel.

By M. Fields. ROCKVILLE, SATURDAY MORNING, AUGUST 11, 1855. Volume I.—No. 1.

The *Montgomery County Sentinel* was founded in 1855 by Matthew Fields, and while many local newspapers came and went, it was published for 165 years. Shown is a portion of the inaugural issue. Fields was a staunch Southern supporter and made his views known in his paper—so much so that he was twice imprisoned in Washington during the Civil War for disloyalty. (Courtesy of Montgomery History.)

An early undertaking, so to speak, that is still operating started in 1854 when William Ellican Pumphrey, a carpenter who made coffins, became an undertaker; five generations succeeded him. Shown is the company's second place of business around 1890. Most 19th-century funerals were held at home; in 1928, grandson William Reuben Pumphrey Jr. purchased a large West Montgomery Avenue residence, still used as a funeral home today.

St. Mary's Roman Catholic Church boasts Rockville's earliest church building, dating to 1817. This sketch depicts its original appearance. In 1890, the current steeple was added, and an 1898 renovation and vestibule addition brought it to how it looks today. With construction of a 1967 sanctuary next door, this building became the parish's chapel but was threatened with demolition, leading to the creation of the Historic District Commission to preserve areas of historic or architectural value. (Courtesy of St. Mary's Church.)

Five other denominations—Baptist, Episcopal, Methodist, Presbyterian, and Disciples of Christ— had an early presence in Rockville. This is the Baptists' second church, built in 1864 on the western edge of town where an earlier church stood since 1823; the small cemetery at Jefferson and Van Buren Streets is the only reminder.

The Methodists' first church, built about 1858, was attended by whites and blacks, although the latter sat in the balcony or stood outside in protest. In 1863, this separatism and the issue of slavery split the congregation, with white members forming a separate church. By 1867, black congregants had acquired the original Wood Lane church. Renamed Jerusalem Methodist Episcopal in 1881, it was dismantled a decade later and, with the same bricks, rebuilt slightly larger, as shown here. The steeple was removed in the 1950s, and the building was given a stucco veneer. Since a 1989 merger, it has been known as Jerusalem–Mount Pleasant United Methodist Church.

Presbyterians built this church—their third—about 1873 after a fire destroyed an earlier one on the same spot facing the Red Brick Courthouse. Their first church, built in 1832, was at Jefferson and Adams Streets. This was one of several buildings razed for construction of the 1931 Grey Courthouse. The current stone Presbyterian church in the West End preserved this building's rose window—placed front and center in both edifices.

Outside Rockville were mills serving surrounding farms. Veirs Mill (pictured) stood where the namesake road crosses Rock Creek. Samuel C. Veirs (whose nearby house was called Meadow Hall, the name of a Rockville school today) built the mill in 1838; it operated until the 1920s, when this photograph was taken. Wootton's Mill, on Watts Branch, operated from 1821 to 1919. Family ancestor Thomas S. Wootton introduced the 1776 bill creating Montgomery County; a high school bears his name.

This painting, "My Old Mill, Holmescroft, Near Rockville," shows Wootton's Mill after it closed. The artist, William Holmes, owned the property and lived in the miller's house when he was director of what is now the Smithsonian American Art Museum in the 1920s. (Courtesy of the Smithsonian Institution.)

NAMES OF SLAVE OWNERS	Number of Slaves	Age	Sex	Colour	Fugitives from the State	Number manumitted	Deaf & dumb, blind, insane, or idiotic
Leonard W. Candler	1	20	M	B			
	1	50	F	M			
	1	10	F	B			
Richard J Bowie	1	21	M	B			
	1	12	M	B			
	1	4	M	M			
	1	2	M	M			
	1	6/12	M	B			
	1	1/12	M	M			
	1	62	F	B			
	1	24	F	M			
	1	18	F	B			
	1	16	F	B			
	1	8	F	B			
Julius West	1	40	M	M			
	1	21	M	B			
	1	15	M	B			
Samuel C Vers	1	63	M	B			
	1	17	M	B			
	1	70	F	B			
	1	13	F	B			
John M Spates	1	9	M	B			
William V Bowie	1	50	M	M			
	1	33	M	B			
	1	50	F	M			
	1	8	F	B			
	1	6	F	B			
George R Braddock	1	55	M	B			
	1	45	F	B			
John G England	1	25	M	B			
	1	19	M	B			
	1	6/12	M	M			
	1	26	F	M			
	1	7	F	M			

Slavery figured significantly in Rockville's early history; above is a portion of the first page of the 1850 US Census Slave Schedule for Rockville. Listed by owner, the enslaved are not named, only described by age, gender, and "color"—B for black, M for "mulatto." Among owners listed, community leader and later chief judge of Maryland's highest court Richard Johns Bowie (right) had the most—11. A subsequent page lists 40 slaves owned by Upton Beall's three daughters, who inherited his property; by the Civil War, they were among the five largest slave owners in the county with 52. Nonetheless, Bowie and the Bealls opposed secession; Union general George McClellan even stayed one night in the Bealls' house on his way to the 1862 Antietam battle—the bloodiest day in American history. (Above, courtesy of the National Archives and Records Administration; right, courtesy of Montgomery History.)

$500 REWARD.—Ran away on Sunday night, the 23d instant, before 12 o'clock, from the subscriber, residing in Rockville, Montgomery county, Md., my NEGRO GIRL "Ann Maria Weems," about 15 years of age; a bright mulatto; some small freckles on her face; slender person, thick suit of hair, inclined to be sandy. Her parents are free, and reside in Washington, D. C. It is evident she was taken away by some one in a carriage, probably by a white man, by whom she may be carried beyond the limits of the State of Maryland.

I will give the above reward for her apprehension and detention so that I get her again.

C. M. PRICE.

Two slaves once owned by Adam Robb would become notable: Josiah Henson (see chapter nine) and Ann Maria Weems. After Robb's death, Weems, a teenager, was sold separately from her mother and nearly all her siblings to Charles Price, a Rockville slave trader who later ran a notorious Alexandria, Virginia, slave pen. Prominent abolitionists helped Weems escape in 1855—from in front of the White House, no less—dressed as a male carriage driver, prompting Price to place ads in the *Sentinel* and even the *Baltimore Sun* (above) offering an unusually high reward. Weems's story is known because she was also aided by William Still, a Philadelphia abolitionist whose 1872 book *The Underground Rail Road* documents many escapes, including others from Rockville. The below illustration of her in disguise is from the book, considered one of the best accounts of the secretive network. (Above, courtesy of Maryland State Archives.)

Rockville experienced military action periodically during the Civil War—with two events tied to important battles. Confederate troops led by Gen. J.E.B. Stuart spent Sunday, June 28, 1863, in Rockville, being cheered by Southern sympathizers, capturing a group of Unionists, plundering farms for provisions and horses, and most importantly, delaying his arrival until well into the crucial battle at Gettysburg, perhaps contributing to the rebels' defeat. Then in 1864, skirmishes between blue and gray soldiers occurred in Rockville before and after the Confederates' unsuccessful advance on the nation's capital at Fort Stevens. (Courtesy of the National Archives and Records Administration.)

These community leaders epitomized the tangle of local sympathies and divisions during the Civil War. William Veirs Bouic Sr. (left), a slave-owning Southern loyalist, was apprehended by Union authorities and imprisoned in Washington; threatened with hanging, he was saved by a friend—Union general George McClelland. John Higgins was one of the Unionists captured by Stuart (as was Richard Johns Bowie, despite being a slaveholder) who were then marched 10 miles away before being freed. Despite their differences, Bouic and Higgins were town commissioners and usually in accord on town business matters.

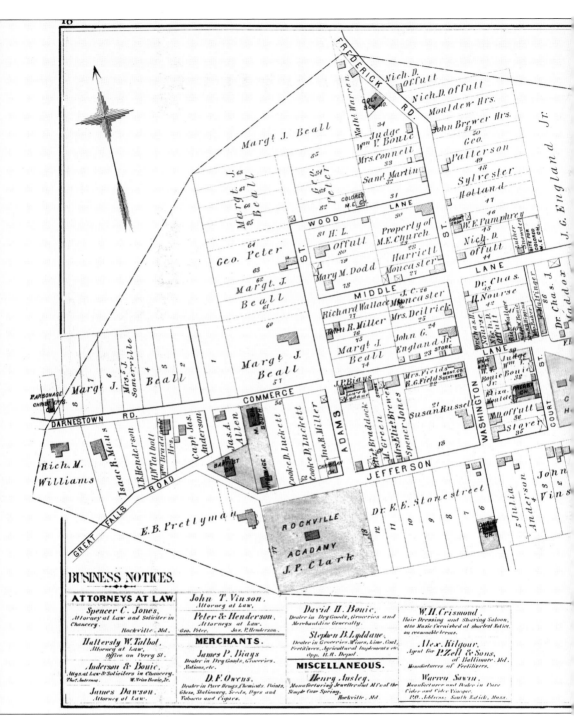

This map from G.M. Hopkins's 1879 "Atlas of Fifteen Miles around Washington including the County of Montgomery, Maryland" shows Rockville's boundaries when incorporated as a town in 1860. The 1840 courthouse is prominently situated in the middle of town, with a growing business district along Montgomery Avenue east of it. As the county seat, at least eight attorneys had offices in town. Unusual for this time, a woman—one of Upton Beall's daughters, Margaret—was the

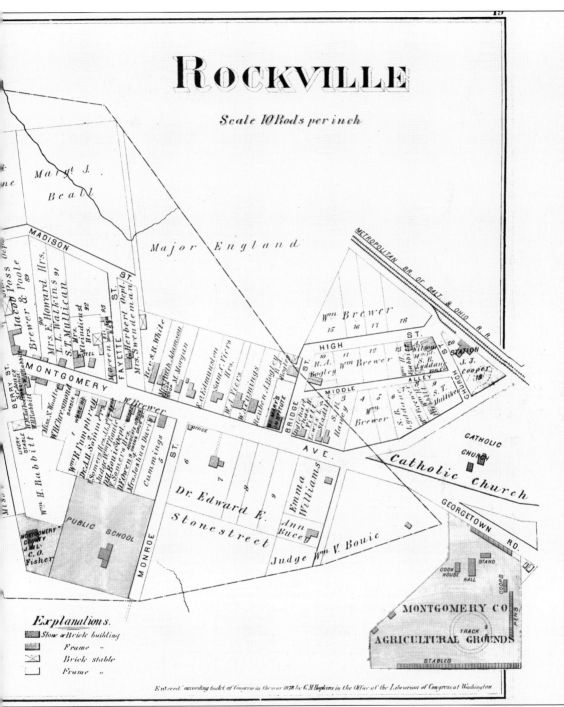

ROCKVILLE

Scale 10 Rods per inch

Marg.t J. Beall

Major England

METROPOLITAN BR. OF BALT & OHIO R.R.

largest landowner, the result of inheritance. Besides community components previously highlighted, there were four schools—a public grade school, "col'd" school for black children, and separate private schools for boys and girls. A large fairground was just outside town. The population had increased to just under 700, largely because of what is shown at far right—a branch line of the Baltimore & Ohio Railroad (B&O)—setting the stage for further change.

These two images nicely capture 19th-century Rockville. The buildings in the c. 1900 photograph at left stood on Montgomery Avenue, already becoming Rockville's main business street. The dormered building was a residence, but the leftmost building was likely a shop or office. The men are standing behind a hitching post. The panoramic view below, photographed about a decade after the Civil War, shows a rustic townscape and rural environs. Much of the foreground area is now largely occupied by Rockville Town Square.

Two

TRANSPORTATION'S
IMPORTANCE

As Rockville began as a crossroads village, transportation is almost a genetic part of the locality, and transportation in various modes molded Rockville into the city it is today.

Just as its location on important early thoroughfares sparked growth, Rockville was affected even more by the train. In 1873, the Baltimore & Ohio Railroad—the nation's first rail carrier—opened a branch line from Washington, DC, through Rockville, making it more accessible and transforming the sleepy little town into a suburb of the nation's capital. Speculators bought close-in farm parcels, carving them up as home lots. Fashionable homes appeared; resort hotels beckoned city dwellers.

"This is the season to make real estate investments about the county seat of Montgomery County," urged one speculator in an 1890 promotional booklet showcasing Rockville's finest homes along with its churches and businesses. Titled *Peerless Rockville*, it proclaimed that "Rockville stands without a rival."

In just two decades, Rockville's population more than doubled to 1,568. In 1900, the trolley was extended from Bethesda (connecting there to DC), fueling more growth. Roughly three decades later, an airport even opened.

But the mode of transportation that shaped Rockville the most was the automobile, turning it into a city in its own right. The turnpike to Georgetown that gave rise to Rockville was paved in 1925; by midcentury, it was rapidly becoming a multilane commercial mecca. The airport had given way to a large shopping center, and the bustling Rockville Pike became a big part of the city's identity.

It also drained activity from the in-town commercial core; a new interstate highway to the west and bypass on the east, both built in the 1950s, also left the downtown struggling. Rescue, for better or worse, came in the form of urban renewal (remembered in chapter eight).

As it turned out, Rockville was eventually reinvigorated in part through the arrival of yet another means of transportation, the regional Metrorail public transit system, in 1984.

The 1873 Rockville railroad station was the largest on the B&O Metropolitan Branch that ran from Washington and then connected with the main line about 25 miles to the northwest. The picturesque Victorian station was later used as a prototype by the Atlas Model Railroad Company for its hobby train sets.

The extension of the Metro Red Line in the 1980s threatened the train station with demolition, but a concerted community effort saved it. In 1981, it was pivoted and moved about 150 feet; now restored, it is used as professional offices.

In 1900, a trolley line was extended to Rockville, solidifying it as a suburb of the nation's capital. Note the cow-catcher at the front of the car above; it was needed as it traversed mainly farming areas, as seen below. The 1910 photograph shows a trolley heading south after diverging from the Rockville Pike. The location is between where Montrose Parkway and Old Georgetown Road meet the pike today.

Until the mid-1920s the Rockville Pike, originally a toll turnpike, was unpaved, mostly ran through countryside, had little traffic, and certainly no stoplights. It became the first road in the county to be paved in 1925, as seen here; the process, involving horse and wagon, bespeaks of one transportation age literally paving the way for another. Despite the coming dominance of cars, the pike would still be just two lanes until 1957. (Courtesy of Montgomery History.)

The automobile's impact on Rockville was tremendous, although this 1931 traffic jam in front of the Red Brick Courthouse was atypical. The cars were likely waiting at the first traffic light, installed just four years earlier at the crossroads.

Reed Brothers Dodge—one of the automaker's first franchised car dealerships in the nation, opening in 1915—was a longtime presence on the prominent triangle formed by the Rockville Pike and Veirs Mill Road. Also the first Gulf gas station in the DC area, it was a three-generation business for 97 years. Founder Lewis Reed, an avid photographer, took many of the photographs in this book; this one, contributed by his granddaughter, shows gas pumps typical of the 1930s. Note the gas price. (Courtesy of Jeanne Gartner.)

Buses replaced the trolley when it ceased service in 1935. Note the lighter pavement in the middle of the road where trolley tracks had been. This is East Montgomery Avenue, once Rockville's main street, running through the core retail district from Courthouse Square to the Rockville Pike and Veirs Mill Road. It and all the stores fronting on it were eliminated in the 1960s urban renewal project. (Roy Perry collection.)

Two less common means of transportation—motorcycles and airplanes—came to Rockville in the 1920s. The 1922 photograph above shows the entire newly formed county police. Six years later, a patrolman crashed into a stopped car on the Rockville Pike and died, becoming the first fallen officer. One of Maryland's largest airfields when it opened in 1928, Congressional Airport offered a school of aeronautics while serving civilian pilots and—it was hoped—congressmen. Pioneering aviatrix Helen Richey—who sometimes teamed with Amelia Earhart in air races—set an international altitude record for a lightweight plane there in 1936. Because of its proximity to the nation's capital, private aircraft could no longer use the airport during World War II; instead, a federally sponsored pilot-training program operated there—the same initiative under which the famous Tuskegee Airmen trained.

Before National (now Reagan) Airport was built in 1941, consideration was given to making Congressional the DC-area commercial airport. Instead, noise complaints and financial troubles led to its closure in the 1950s. The hangar became a roller rink open until 1983, and the landing field became a legendary shopping center, both taking the airport's name.

Congressional Plaza, known for its dazzling neon sign, was one of the county's largest shopping centers when it opened in 1959. It was to be called Congressional Shopping City as an alternative to the downtown commercial district, but officials reduced the proposed 30-acre size by one-third. It included Rockville's first national clothing store, J.C. Penney, its largest grocery at the time (with a sign almost as large), and a G.C. Murphy variety store, which moved from downtown. The plaza's success set the stage for other businesses to line the pike in short order, ultimately to the in-town business district's detriment. (Roy Perry collection.)

Car travel gave rise to a new kind of overnight lodging, motor hotels, which became known as motels. The Rockville Plaza Motor Hotel, located on North Washington Street, opened in 1969 but struggled to lure interstate highway travelers. After about two decades, it was converted into subsidized apartments by a nonprofit housing organization; today, it is the remodeled Beall's Grant complex.

The most recent form of transportation to leave its mark on Rockville came with the extension of Metro in 1984. The downtown station helped bring people back to its central core after the midcentury urban renewal effort was not entirely successful in reviving a declining downtown. (Courtesy of Montgomery History.)

Three

CENTER OF GOVERNMENT

One of Rockville's early names—Montgomery Court House—might aptly be reapplied today, as four courthouses stand prominently in the city, underscoring its association to government, particularly as a judicial center.

The landmark 1891 Red Brick Courthouse serves as the most iconic and well-known symbol of Rockville's role as the seat of county government. Flanking it on either side, and reflecting the county's tremendous growth over the years, are the 1931 Grey Courthouse and the 1982 concrete Montgomery County Circuit Court Building with its numerous courtrooms; the two earlier buildings had only one each. Nearby are towers housing county legislative and administrative functions to complete the picture on the county level.

Since 2011, another courthouse has been part of the cityscape, the Maryland District Court at Jefferson Street and Maryland Avenue, giving state government a presence as well.

As important locally, of course, is city government. Incorporated in 1860, Rockville became self-governing with three commissioners; it adopted its current mayor-and-council form of government in 1888. While town government was quite minimal initially, services increased as Rockville grew to be Maryland's second-largest city by the mid-20th century. A professional city manager position was created in 1948. A slate of reform-minded officials elected a few years later worked toward a more modern, expanded government. And then, in 1955, the state enacted home rule, freeing Rockville and other incorporated municipalities from obtaining state authorization for most matters.

As government increased at all levels, Rockville became very much a government center, symbolically and physically—the numerous courthouses and county office buildings, a modern city hall, and a Depression-era post office building now headquartering the city's police force together fill a large, multi-block area of its downtown, defining it as a place of importance.

After 50 years, the 1840 courthouse was inadequate to handle the increasing county government functions; a new one was built in 1891 on the same spot. The Romanesque building's commanding tower bespoke its importance. Known today as the Red Brick Courthouse to distinguish it from successors, it is perhaps Rockville's most distinctive landmark. The upstairs courtroom, restored to reflect its original grandeur, provides a spot for community forums.

With still more space needed four decades later, the limestone Neoclassical 1931 Grey Courthouse was constructed, adjoining its predecessor. Rockville's biggest construction project to that time, it is seen nearing completion above and on a postcard below soon after opening. In the 1960s, it got an addition on its right side—how it looks today—and the Red Brick Courthouse was threatened with demolition, but citizens' objections saved the iconic building. (Below, courtesy of Montgomery History.)

With much of Montgomery County, like Rockville, booming after World War II, county government functions increased tremendously, necessitating construction of this building in 1953 to house offices that no longer fit in the courthouse. Called simply the County Office Building, it was later named for Stella Werner, a leader of the successful campaign in the early 1940s to replace the county board of commissioners with a manager and seven-member county council. (Courtesy of Montgomery History.)

Stella Werner is seen here with longtime Montgomery County Circuit Court judge Charles W. Woodward Sr. at a radio interview around 1950. That year, she became the second woman elected to the county council and was the first to win reelection—twice. (Courtesy of Montgomery History.)

Needing ever more space, the county constructed yet another courthouse in 1981—its fifth and biggest by far—just beyond the third and fourth; it is shown above under construction and below along with its two predecessors. A companion tower, the Executive Office Building (at right above), was completed earlier in the year. It houses varied departments under the county executive, an elected post created in 1970 to replace the appointed manager. The Werner Building then became offices entirely for the council, the legislative body.

The county jail, located where the county council building now sits, is shown being dismantled in 1931; prisoners were then confined in the Grey Courthouse. In 1880, a 23-year-old black man being held in the jail on suspicion of rape was taken by vigilante groups and lynched about a mile away. Sixteen years later, the same fate befell a 28-year-old black man held for alleged murder. No arrests were made in either incident. The last execution of a convicted criminal by hanging was in 1921. (Courtesy of Montgomery History.)

The county almshouse and poor farm, sheltering indigents, disabled individuals, and others with no means of support, operated from 1789 until 1959, when it was razed for construction of the county detention facility on Seven Locks Road. The remains of many who died there were buried in an adjacent potter's field—Interstate 270 covers most of it. In 1987, thirty-eight bodies on the other side of the highway were exhumed and moved to Parklawn Cemetery.

For town government, one of the first major projects was development of a municipal water system in 1898, replacing private wells. Rockville dug its own well, and water was delivered from this pumping station still standing in Croydon Park (now remodeled as a community center). The facility also supplied electricity. A typhoid outbreak during the 1913 Christmas season, traced to contamination of the public well, spurred development of a sewage system.

Explosive growth after World War II brought on a water shortage—with severe usage restrictions—that ultimately was solved by tapping the Potomac River, still the city's supply. This also led to the election of reform-minded candidates pledging to modernize city government. Dedicating the $2.6 million water system in 1958, officials took a celebratory drink at a water fountain in front of the Grey Courthouse.

While city officials were dealing with the water shortage and other issues brought on by rapid growth, they also decided to buy a mansion as a "public country club" and site for cultural events. Glenview Mansion, shown above in the 1920s, was originally the more modest 19th-century farmhouse of Richard Johns Bowie, depicted in the illustration below. It was owned in the early to mid-1900s by a wealthy Washington couple named Lyon who remodeled and enlarged it, first adding the wing on the right above and then a similar one on the left (how it looks today). The Montgomery County Historical Society purchased it in 1954 but struggled to maintain it; Rockville bought it three years later. (Below, courtesy of City of Rockville.)

Added to the Glenview property in 1960 was the Civic Auditorium, which evolved into the F. Scott Fitzgerald Theatre, and the entire complex took on its present name—Rockville Civic Center Park. The final piece was the addition of the adjacent Croydon Creek Nature Center and adjoining 120-acre John G. Hayes Forest Preserve in 2000.

City government operated out of this house from 1954 to 1962, when the present city hall was constructed on the site at a cost of just under $250,000 for an 18,000-square-foot building; subsequent additions and renovations have resulted in how it appears today.

Although Rockville replaced its three commissioners with the mayor and council, a five-member governing body, in 1888, it was nearly a century before the title "councilwoman" was needed. In 1972, Jean Horneck, a former city clerk, became the first woman elected to the council. In 1984, Viola Hovsepian (left) was selected by her fellow council members to fill the unexpired term of a mayor who resigned, thus being the first woman appointed mayor. The first woman elected in her own right to the position was Rose Krasnow (below) in 1995—also the first woman elected mayor of a comparably sized city in Maryland. She was twice reelected, serving until 2001. As mayor, she led a process dubbed Imagine Rockville that envisioned much of today's Rockville Town Center. (Left, courtesy of Montgomery History.)

The city offered its first summer recreation programs in 1948; in 1959 came a teen center (pictured) within walking distance of Richard Montgomery High School. This building, greatly remodeled, is now the Elwood Smith Community Center. Named for a firefighter who died trying to rescue occupants of a submerged car, it is one of numerous community/recreation centers run by the city that offer programs for all ages. Beginning in the early 1970s, activities for seniors were offered in the pump house and elsewhere; the Rockville Senior Center opened in 1982 in the former Woodley Gardens Elementary School.

The Rockville Municipal Swim Center opened in 1968. Originally only this outdoor pool, it has been greatly expanded over the years and now includes a larger outdoor pool, two indoor pools, two recreational pools, a tot pool, and a spiral water flume. The swim and teen centers were both designed by prolific local architect John H. Sullivan, known for many mid-20th-century Modern buildings in Rockville. (Courtesy of City of Rockville.)

**ROCKVILLE, MARYLAND
ALL-AMERICA CITY**

*The Mayor and Council of Rockville
Cordially Invite You and Your Family
To Attend All-America City Day
From 12 noon to 4:00 p.m.
Sunday, May 6, at the Rockville Civic Center
To Celebrate the City's All-America City Award
To Be Presented at 1:45 p.m.*

Rockville is a four-time recipient of the All-America City award presented by the National Civic League, winning in 1954, 1961, 1977, and 1979. On the occasion of its fourth award—at the time the only city to be so honored in the contest's history—residents were invited to a gala celebration. The award recognizes communities that leverage civic engagement, collaboration, inclusiveness, and innovation to successfully address local issues.

In 1960, anti-segregation activists pointed out the incongruity between the All-America honor and racial restrictions in some local restaurants; they distributed fliers urging boycotts of offending establishments. Taking more direct action, 25 people were arrested later that year at a sit-in at a HiBoy restaurant to protest its policy of serving black customers only carry-out items. The action came just five months after a Greensboro, North Carolina, lunch counter sit-in attracted national attention. (Courtesy of Montgomery History.)

STOP!

•

We are asking your support in an effort to bring real democracy to Rockville.

Rockville has won an award as an All-American City
We Are Proud Of This Award. We Know You Are.

*   *   *

This store will not serve ALL OF ITS CUSTOMERS AT ITS FOOD COUNTERS will you help us to change this policy and make this truly an **ALL-AMERICAN CITY,** a wonderful place in which to live.

Shop at stores like **Murphy's** that serve everyone alike.

**Montgomery Civic Unity Committee
V. F. W. Post 9863
N A A C P Rockville Branch**

The 1939 dedication of Rockville's first permanent post office, a federal New Deal project, included a parade, concert, and speeches but also a protestor. Matthew Fields's *Sentinel* office once stood on the site; granddaughter Elizabeth Wimsatt planted a "no trespassing" sign to dramatize her claim that she was not compensated for the land. She also used a hatchet to ward off a postal official who suffered a cut hand in their altercation. (Courtesy of the Library of Congress.)

This 2006 ceremony marked the post office's closing, but just six years later, it was rededicated as the city's police station, saving a historic building and mural depicting Sugarloaf Mountain, a natural landmark not quite visible from Rockville. In 2019, the work of art was chosen as one of five reproduced on postage stamps commemorating Depression-era murals once adorning post offices nationwide.

Vivian Simpson (left) opened a law practice in Rockville in 1928, becoming the county's first woman attorney. In 1949, Gov. William Preston Lane (right) appointed her Maryland's first female secretary of state, but she resigned after about a year, saying she was "too independent" to be at others' "beck and call." In 2004, she was posthumously inducted into the Maryland Women's Hall of Fame.

Rockville and Pinneburg, Germany, became Sister Cities in 1957, one of the most enduring such relationships in the world. This wreath presentation ceremony at the Red Brick Courthouse marked its beginning. In 2019, Rockville and Yilan City, Taiwan, also became Sister Cities, and in 2009, Rockville began an informal relationship with Jizxing, China; the city established a nonprofit organization in 1986 to enhance inclusion of Rockville's diverse cultural communities through the Sister City program.

Four

EDUCATION IN
BLACK AND WHITE

As the county seat, Rockville led the way in terms of education—but as elsewhere, racially segregated schools were a big part of the story.

One of the county's first educational ventures came in the early 19th century with establishment of the Rockville Academy, essentially a private school for the wealthy. Public schooling came about a half century later; a one-room schoolhouse opened just beyond the town line—one of the first in the county and several years before Maryland set up a statewide public education system. Previous attempts to create public schools were never sufficiently funded; a new state constitution in 1864 mandated a "uniform system of free public schools" that finally took hold, but initially only for white children.

Although that constitution abolished slavery, little consideration was given to educating black children until eight years later, when the state mandated they also be provided schooling, but in separate facilities. Locally, with assistance from the Freedmen's Bureau, a federal post–Civil War reconstruction agency with a county office in Rockville, the black community held school in the Methodist church basement in 1867, and perhaps earlier. The county finally built a "colored" school in Rockville in 1876, the same year a new school for white students opened that was not only larger but had an assembly hall, a rarity at the time.

Other educational milestones included the first high school in the county—though for whites only. A black high school would not open until 35 years later, and there would be only one in the entire county over the next three decades. In many ways, it was "secondary" education indeed, with hand-me-down books and less funding per student than for the dozen or so white high schools, but with dedicated black teachers who made half what white teachers with the same credentials earned. Teacher William B. Gibbs Jr. sued the county over the salary issue with the help of Thurgood Marshall, a young lawyer who would become the 20th century's most-renowned African American litigator.

The community's first school, the Rockville Academy, dates from 1805 when Maryland's legislature passed a law appointing seven leading Rockville citizens to raise $2,500 by lottery for construction of a schoolhouse. However, it primarily served only children (mainly boys) whose families could afford its tuition. Educational opportunities for girls were generally more limited and were provided by the Rockville Female Seminary, St. Mary's Institute, and private tutors.

With a bequest from farmer-attorney Julius West, for whom a middle school is named, this structure replaced the academy's original building in 1890. The school lasted only two and a half decades longer, closing in 1916 due to financial difficulties—despite admitting girls just four years earlier. This still-standing building housed public school students until 1935 and then served about three decades as Rockville's library.

Rockville's first one-room public school, about 1861, was replaced in 1876 by a four-room structure (above) that was larger than any public school in the county at the time. Both were only for white children. Also in 1876, a one-room school for black children (below) was erected—four years after Maryland had mandated public education be provided to African Americans. An earlier black school nonetheless existed by 1867, established through grassroots efforts by Rockville's black community, made up of previously free and newly emancipated individuals eager to educate their children.

Montgomery County High School, built in 1905, was the county's first. Secondary schooling began in 1892 with a two-room addition to Rockville's grade school for white students, allowing courses beyond seventh grade to be taught. Twelfth grade did not come about until the mid-1920s. As other high schools began opening around the county, this school was informally called Rockville High School.

This photograph, taken shortly after construction of the high school, shows how bucolic Rockville was even into the 20th century. The building stood in part of what is now Americana Centre. Note the Red Brick Courthouse tower on the left. (Courtesy of Jeanne Gartner.)

The high school was overcrowded from the very start. Just when it was completed, the grade school burned down, forcing all grades to be squeezed into the new building. It was enlarged several times, barely accommodating ever-increasing numbers of students. Stopgap measures included holding some classes in a nearby hotel and the Rockville Academy after it closed.

A fire gutted the building in 1940. Officials scrambled to place students in other high schools until a new school was built two years later. By this time, it had officially been renamed Richard Montgomery High School (RMHS), making it the oldest of the numerous high schools around the county today.

The 1876 Rockville Colored School got a second story in 1891. The school burned down in 1912 and was replaced—but not until 1921—with a building (visible in the background) hardly larger than the previous school. In 1927, the structure added in front became the first high school for African Americans. The buildings, which shared one bathroom, were constructed with partial funding from Sears president Julius Rosenwald, whose generosity helped build nearly 5,000 black public schools throughout the segregated South. (Courtesy of Montgomery History.)

In 1937, Rockville teacher William B. Gibbs Jr. sued the county over its practice of paying black teachers about half what similarly qualified white teachers earned. To avoid a trial, the county agreed to equalize salaries over a two-year period. However, Gibbs was fired, ostensibly because he was not qualified to also serve as principal, as he had been. In 2009, the county named a school for him, and a Rockville street now bears his name. The case reinvigorated the local chapter of the NAACP, which is still active today. Gibbs's attorney Thurgood Marshall was especially noteworthy (see chapter nine).

With Rockville Colored High School the only one for black students in the entire county, getting to school was difficult for many, especially since the county did not initially provide transportation. By the time the first class graduated (shown posing with the principal on the left), the black community had pooled resources to purchase a bus, driven by one of the students.

Rockville Colored High School was soon overcrowded. In 1935, this building opened as Lincoln High School; however, it was still the only one in the county for black students. It is believed to have been moved from Takoma Park and faced with bricks to match the white high schools then being built. Soon overcrowded too, a wooden addition was built by industrial arts students. After World War II, Quonset huts were placed out back for additional space. (Courtesy of Montgomery History.)

In 1935, Rockville Elementary School (above) was built near the fairground, about where the first one-room public school had been. Constructed with New Deal assistance, the impressive Georgian-style edifice became the city's first junior high school in the 1950s. It was razed in the early 2000s to make way for a replacement of the building below—the "new" Richard Montgomery High—which was built in 1940 to replace the 1905 school destroyed by fire. Its design projected an "air of modernity" that was reinforced by the school symbol, a rocket. The building was added onto several times; additions in the 1960s and 1980s significantly altered its appearance. However it is remembered, it was a Rockville landmark for generations who attended. The third RMHS, constructed in 2005–2007, sits on the football field of this building, which was once the fairground's oval track. (Both, courtesy of Montgomery History.)

As baby boomers reached school age in the early 1950s, elementary schools were being built in Rockville one after another. Above is West Rockville Elementary, which now has been renovated and renamed Beall. The others, Lone Oak, Rock Terrace, Twinbrook, Maryvale, and Meadow Hall, were followed by eight more in the 1960s and early 1970s. The ensuing "baby bust" resulted in agonizing closure of some—even a few newer ones. It was not until 2018 that another elementary school was built in Rockville.

Broome Junior High School was built in 1957 to accommodate seventh-through-ninth-grade students who swelled elementary school enrollments just a few years earlier. Named for Rockville resident Edwin Broome, who served nearly four decades as county school superintendent, it was designed by local architect Rhees Burkett in the contemporary International style, combining long sleek bands of windows with brick, stone, and metal. (RB photograph.)

In 1950, a modern high school, generally on par with white facilities, was built for black students and doubled as a junior college. Above is Carver High School's class of 1954, which graduated just as the Supreme Court overturned school segregation; the class of 1960 was the school's last. With desegregation, the building became the school system's headquarters, and its name was retained to commemorate its earlier use. Nearby Rock Terrace Elementary (below) was one of four black grade schools built around the county in the early 1950s that also were comparable to their white counterparts, largely ending the use of one- and two-room wooden schools for African Americans in the mid-20th century. After desegregation, it became a special needs school. (Below, RB photograph.)

Two Rockville schools are seen here in black and white. Above is a 1956 sixth-grade class at Lone Oak Elementary; below is a 1957 class at Rock Terrace. Desegregation of the county's schools was a gradual process, beginning in 1956 and extending to 1961.

The Rockville campus of Montgomery College—then a junior college—began to take shape in early 1965; classes commenced that September. Maryland's first community college, it started as a night school at Bethesda–Chevy Chase High School in 1946, then moved to Takoma Park in 1950, taking over a defunct trade school. Rockville was its second campus. What is now Interstate 270 is just visible in the upper left; built in 1957, it was then only two lanes in each direction. (Courtesy of Montgomery History.)

The college was built on the farm of the Andersons, a longtime Rockville family. Among the structures razed was this log cabin. This photograph, a reminder of the farms that once surrounded the city, serves as an apt visual bookend to two centuries of schooling in Rockville. (Courtesy of Montgomery History.)

Five

TAKING CARE OF BUSINESS

Although Rockville derives much of its identity from being the seat of Montgomery County, commercial enterprise has been a big part of its history, especially as the Rockville Pike boomed as a region-wide shopping mecca.

The photographs on the following pages depicting business activity seek to underscore the ways in which Rockville stands out as, well, "peerless" in this aspect of community life. Businesses common to most communities thrived here, of course, but there were others that were hardly run of the mill.

Besides the *Sentinel*, other newspapers existed for varying lengths of time to cover Rockville and county government. One of the county's most prolific architects plied his trade from an office/residence that he designed and built in the heart of Rockville. Banks especially thrived, with one issuing a tidy sum of paper money bearing its name, Montgomery County National Bank of Rockville. With the train and then trolley providing Washington residents ready access, Rockville hotels became resort destinations; the grandest one later became the preeminent psychiatric hospital Chestnut Lodge.

The county's only drive-in movie theater was in Rockville, and the in-town theater, which opened as the Milo in 1935 and was later the Villa, had the rare opportunity to show a 1964 film partly shot in the city that even included a shot of the cinema itself—*Lilith*, based on a novel set in Chestnut Lodge and starring Warren Beatty, Jean Seberg, Peter Fonda, and Gene Hackman, who acted out some scenes on location in Rockville (see chapter nine).

And a popular DC metropolitan area radio station once beamed out rock and roll hits from a studio in the heart of Rockville.

Vinson's Pharmacy, the corner store that prominently stood diagonally across from the Red Brick Courthouse, was as much a community gathering spot as a business. Built in 1886, it was an earlier pharmacy that was acquired in 1901 by "Doc Willie" Vinson, who operated it until his 1958 death. The building was then replaced by a three-story modern office building that stood only a decade until urban renewal. (Courtesy of Montgomery History.)

Vinson's soda fountain, which introduced frosty, creamy drinks to residents, today graces the meeting room of Rockville Memorial Library, courtesy of Peerless Rockville. When installed in the store in 1914, the *Sentinel* described it as unsurpassed "by anything of its kind in Washington city . . . for beauty, cost and modern style." (Sketch by Gary Funkhouser.)

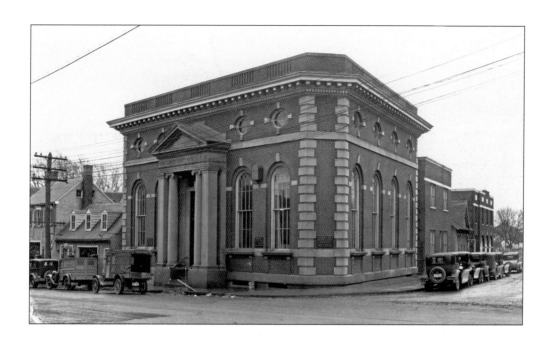

This stately edifice, located across from Vinson's on East Montgomery Avenue, was Montgomery County National Bank of Rockville. Like other federally chartered banks, it was allowed to print currency. From 1884 until 1935, it printed $2.7 million in various denominations; its series 1929 $20 bill is shown below. Issuance of more than $1 million is considered significant, as is the bank's half-century-long printing period. The widespread practice ended when the Federal Reserve System standardized paper money. This 1905 building—the work of prominent Baltimore architect E. Francis Baldwin, who also designed the train station—was one of the most striking in Rockville's business district demolished for urban renewal; it stood where the Montgomery County Circuit Court building stands. The bank started in the building next to Vinson's (pictured in the above photograph on the opposite page, then occupied by the *Sentinel*), another handsome structure razed.

Rockville has had a number of striking bank buildings. Farmers Banking and Trust Company, founded in 1900, had just moved into this Art Deco building—the city's only surviving example—when this 1931 photograph was taken. Across the street is the construction site of the Grey Courthouse, completed the same year; the earlier, smaller Farmers bank had been on the site.

Suburban Trust's Rockville branch on North Washington Street—commonly known as the pink bank building—was a fine example of mid-20th-century Modern architecture. It was a prestigious address; among those with offices in the building was Vivian Simpson, the county's first woman attorney. Despite efforts to save it, the structure was demolished in 2014, fifty years after it was constructed. (Courtesy of the Library of Congress.)

As the county's judicial and civic center, Rockville has always housed numerous lawyers' offices. Pictured is the office of Hattersley Talbott and Charles Prettyman, located appropriately on Court Street, a short but prestigious roadway next to the Red Brick Courthouse and eliminated by the Grey Courthouse.

In the mid-20th century, Perry Street (now Maryland Avenue) was known informally as lawyers' row because of the attorneys' offices that lined the street. The buildings faced the east side of the Red Brick Courthouse, then still being used for court business along with the Grey Courthouse. At far left was Montgomery County National Bank, three buildings to the right was the fire station, and at far right was a Chesapeake & Potomac Telephone Company building.

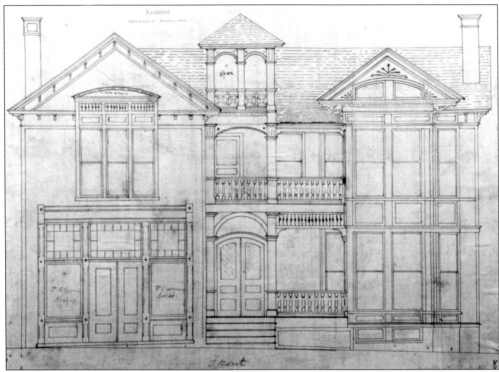

Architect Thomas C. Groomes lived in a house with an adjoining office, depicted in this blueprint, that he designed and built for himself in 1888. It stood prominently in the center of Rockville; Farmers bank was constructed next to it in 1931. Groomes designed the 1905 high school and many prominent Rockville residents' homes in the late 1800s and early 1900s. His wife, Agnes, operated Rockville's first telephone exchange on the first floor of their house; she was considered among the town's best-informed residents. The building can also be seen in the cover photograph but with a different facade to modernize it. (Below, Roy Perry collection.)

To a certain extent, hoteliers prospered in Rockville. Montgomery House (pictured in chapter one) and the Corcoran Hotel on East Montgomery Avenue (pictured here on a postcard) first catered to those having courthouse business and then flourished during Rockville's resort era when trains and trolleys brought city dwellers seeking a rural respite. The Corcoran was later carved up into shops seeking a presence on the city's main street, adding to the hodgepodge appearance the business district took on by the mid-1900s.

Rockville's grandest resort hotel was the Woodlawn in the West End; however, it operated only from 1889 until 1906, when the owners, heavily in debt, sold it. A psychiatrist, Dr. Ernest L. Bullard, opened it as a sanitarium in 1910. Under his son Dexter, it became one of the first mental hospitals in the world specializing in the new field of psychoanalysis. This intriguing story continues in chapter nine.

The hardware store is an American icon; these two photographs dramatically show how it has evolved over the years. Note the New Deal–era sign for the National Recovery Administration (above) patriotically displayed by Rockville Paint and Hardware, located on East Montgomery Avenue. Hechinger (below), a mid-20th-century Washington-area pioneering chain of do-it-yourself home improvement stores, was characterized by its striking futuristic architecture and distinctive roofline of diamond shapes. The store was on Hungerford Drive at North Washington Street, the site of a Giant grocery today.

The structure that housed Wire Hardware survives today as an office building. The brick building, located behind St. Mary's cemetery (at right), has housed several businesses over the years. This 1943 photograph shows it when it was a general store run by Porter and Frank Ward. Built in 1895 by William Wallace Welsh for the same purpose (along with his residence next door), its location next to the train station assured its success. (Roy Perry collection.)

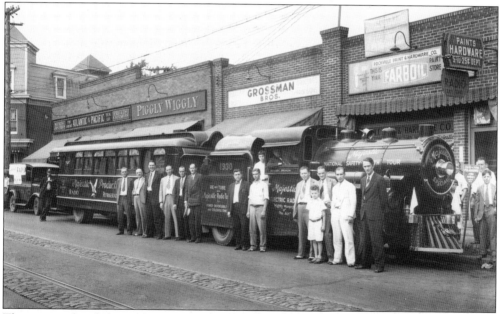

This is not a derailed train but a traveling promotion for Majestic radios, which debuted in 1930. Perhaps more interesting is that Rockville then had three food stores right next to each other—Atlantic & Pacific and Piggly Wiggly groceries and a local entity, Grossman Bros. meat market. Besides Grossman, several other Jewish families owned Rockville stores; when they closed for Jewish holidays, the *Sentinel* published explanatory articles for the predominately Protestant town.

Rockville's black community maintained a variety of commercial enterprises, mostly in Lincoln Park and the Washington Street–Middle Lane area. For about 50 years, Mr. T's restaurant and store served as much as a community institution as a business. It is seen here in the late 1960s, shortly before being replaced by a North Washington Street gas station. Proprietor George Jackson was the first black member of the Rockville Chamber of Commerce.

Around the corner from Mr. T's was a thriving printing business that husband and wife Jesse and Celestine Hebron ran for many years out of their concrete-block home, which is still standing on Wood Lane. Jesse Hebron started the business in a shop elsewhere in 1932, built the house after serving in World War II—even molding the blocks on-site himself—then continued operations from their basement for the next 50 years.

Dating to 1926 and the only remaining black business in the North Washington Street area is Snowden Funeral Home, still family-run four generations later. Founder George Russell Snowden gave funerals a stately air with a hearse drawn by four white horses. A later motorized, but equally stately, hearse used by the company is shown here. The Snowdens have been active in community affairs, and in 1985 the family received an NAACP award for community awareness, citizenship, and human kindness. (Courtesy of Montgomery History.)

The black business district, the Rockville colored elementary school, and a largely African American neighborhood and church were all replaced by this strip mall in the early 1950s. Located diagonally across North Washington Street from Snowden Funeral Home, "one stop" Rockville Center was the city's largest when it opened in 1957 but was dwarfed by Congressional Plaza two years later. Pictured in the early 1970s when anchored by W.T. Grant, it was known later for the Magruder's grocery located there. (Roy Perry collection.)

Farming in and around Rockville continued well into the 20th century. Dawson Farm Park off Ritchie Parkway is just a portion of a large farm that extended from the pike to what is now Interstate 270. During the Civil War, Lawrence Dawson, who owned three slaves but was a Union Army enrollment officer, was one of those captured by J.E.B. Stuart. Following a nearby skirmish, his wife, Mary, nursed wounded soldiers on both sides. Dawson family members pose in front of the 1874 farmhouse (above); it was saved from demolition by Peerless Rockville in 1983 after falling into disrepair. A grander adjacent farmhouse (below) was built in 1912; both border the park.

Also still standing within Rockville are this barn and farmhouse, pictured around 1975. Presently located at Woodmont Country Club, they were once owned by the Lyddane family in the late 19th century. In the early 1900s, the farm belonged to a Washington couple named Bradley who used it mainly as a summer residence. The country club acquired it in 1950 and sold its previous Bethesda site to the neighboring National Institutes of Health. The house, painted white in the style of other grand summer homes along the Rockville Pike, has been returned to its natural brick appearance. (Below, courtesy of Montgomery County Planning Department.)

The Milo Theatre, located opposite Courthouse Square, was a popular downtown spot. Although this 1945 photograph shows black and white patrons lined up together to purchase tickets, the former had to enter a rear door and sit in the balcony.

Rockville Drive-In Theatre had a 17-year run, closing in 1981. Shown is an ad for opening day, March 18, 1954. However, over a foot of snow delayed the opening for one week. The county's only drive-in, the popular attraction was located off Hungerford Drive near Carver High School, the site of the townhouse community on Ivy League Lane today. Like the Milo, it was segregated in its early years.

WINX Radio, one of several DC-area 1960s-era Top 40 stations, blasted out the latest rock and roll hits from a very old spot—a historic residence on Hungerford Drive just north of St. Mary's cemetery. Neither the station nor the building (once the home of Mayor Lee Offutt) exists today—ironically, it is the site of a retirement community where a former listener or two may reside.

Prominent announcers who got their start at WINX included Jack Diamond, a morning host on Washington's WRQX for nearly three decades; the fast-talking Barry Richards—"the boss with the hot sauce"—who later was a consultant to Alice Cooper and Led Zeppelin, among others; and Bob Duckman, who has logged more than 50 years on the air, including more than a decade on DC's WASH and, since 2004, on Annapolis radio. Duckman is seen here in a WINX jacket, which he proudly noted still fit decades later. (Courtesy of Bob Duckman.)

The early 1950s photograph above shows a thriving business district. But just a decade later, as business on the pike and elsewhere siphoned away customers, store vacancies began occurring, and city officials set their sights on revitalization. This streetscape would be replaced by Americana Centre in 1972; to spark business, an indoor shopping mall built roughly opposite the courthouse tower opened at the same time (seen below in 1974). How this urban renewal effort turned out is covered in chapter eight—spoiler alert: the mall was ultimately not successful in taking care of business. (Below, Roy Perry collection.)

Six

COMMUNITY INSTITUTIONS AND TRADITIONS

Rockville residents have a long tradition of banding together to form organizations of all sorts dedicated to community betterment and service.

With local government's reach quite minimal until the mid-20th century, citizen associations and volunteers stepped in to fight fires, operate a library, and provide a community cemetery—with the African American community sometimes leading the way. For general edification and even amusement, Rockville Town Hall (not at all what probably comes to mind) filled the bill. And Rockville hosted a quintessential community institution—the county fair—for decades.

As seen in chapter one, religion took root in Rockville early, and religious institutions have been an important part of community life ever since. The first denominations grew into larger houses of worship while new congregations of these faiths and others began churches, especially with Rockville's explosive growth after World War II. The more recent diversity of Rockville's population is reflected in other congregations devoted to particular cultural and ethnic traditions.

In the 1960s, two separate United Church of Christ and Presbyterian congregations merged as Rockville United Church and formed Community Ministries of Rockville to meet critical social needs; it has been a key part of the city's service network ever since. A health clinic and homeless shelters are among its contributions; reflecting an ever-increasing scope of services in Rockville and beyond, it became Community Reach of Montgomery County, still based in the county seat.

Numerous other service and civic organizations have enhanced community life, including the Rockville Chamber of Commerce and Rotary, Lions, and Kiwanis clubs, just as fraternal organizations remembered in this chapter did in earlier years. And for over a century from its 1900 founding, the Woman's Club of Rockville has been a part of the picture, advocating for wide-ranging reforms, raising money for the Red Cross, and sponsoring Chautauqua programs.

Christ Episcopal Church has been an enduring presence on South Washington Street since 1822—even surviving a powerful 1896 hurricane that severely damaged this building erected just nine years earlier, which is still in use. The congregation first met in a wooden chapel on the grounds of Rockville Cemetery and then built an in-town church on the site of the present one. Although pre–Civil War members included slaveholders, it is rumored a basement hideaway in the 1822 building was a haven on the Underground Railroad for those fleeing slavery.

Rockville Cemetery was originally the Episcopalian burying grounds; its oldest headstone, which belongs to John Harding, who died in 1752, is shown here. After being neglected, it became a community graveyard through the work of an association formed in 1880 and with a donation by Richard Johns Bowie of five acres from his adjacent Glen View farm; his widow, Catharine, later added two more acres. Many notable Rockville and county citizens are interred there. (RB photograph.)

After the Methodists' antebellum split over slavery, white congregants formed Rockville Methodist Episcopal South and built this church on Commerce Lane (now West Montgomery Avenue) about 1869; the tower was not added until 1900. After a 1942 fire, it was expanded, covered with stone, and remains in use.

Freed slaves who initially met at Jerusalem Methodist Episcopal built their own church, Clinton African Methodist Episcopal Zion Church, on Middle Lane about 1870. A larger replacement was destroyed by fire, and in 1904, this brick structure was built nearby on Washington Street; the photograph shows it about a decade before it, as well as much of an adjoining black community, was replaced by the shopping center pictured on page 69. The congregation built a new church in Lincoln Park and remains active today. (Roy Perry collection.)

Rockville Christian (Disciples of Christ) Church formed in 1822; in 1858, the congregation purchased the former Presbyterian meetinghouse at Jefferson and Adams Streets, which it replaced with this structure in 1893. It is no longer used as a church; in 1964, the congregation relocated near Interstate 270 and later opened an adjacent nursing home.

From 1913 until 1974, Rockville Baptist Church, seen in this late 1960s photograph, anchored the corner of Washington and Jefferson Streets about where Hungerford's Tavern was. The congregation's current church is just east of Interstate 270; with the addition of other Baptist congregations in Rockville, it is now First Baptist.

Ten families founded Rockville's first Jewish congregation, Beth Tikva, in 1959. Membership steadily grew, and this Baltimore Road synagogue was built in 1965. Merging with a Silver Spring congregation in 1997, it is now Tikvat Israel. As the city grew rapidly after World War II, many religious institutions blossomed, including Lutheran, Unitarian, Assembly of God, Seventh-day Adventist, and Christian Science churches in the 1950s and 1960s. In 1998, a nondenominational church, Twinbrook Community, formed. (Roy Perry collection.)

More recently, Rockville's churches have increasingly reflected the city's greater multicultural makeup. Many congregations have a diverse membership while others reach out specifically to various ethnicities, particularly those of Hispanic and Asian descent. One such house of worship is East Rockville's First Korean Presbyterian Church of Washington, offering services in Korean and English. (RB photograph.)

St. Mary's Catholic Church opened a school in 1951 that generations of Rockville families attended; above are its 1964 graduating eighth graders. Christ Episcopal also began a school as a church mission in 1966. In much earlier years, edification of a more general sort was provided in a unique community institution. Rockville Town Hall (the building at left below) did not house government offices, as readily comes to mind today; it was built and started in 1881 by citizens seeking to "improve the educational, moral, scientific, literary, and social condition of the community." Located on East Montgomery Avenue next to Vinson's Pharmacy, it served as a venue for lectures, plays, concerts, dances, and other community gatherings. In the 1930s, it was replaced by a G.C. Murphy variety store, which later moved to Congressional Plaza.

At the beginning of the 19th century, fires were fought with a hand-drawn water barrel on wheels by male residents who came running at the sight of smoke. By the next century, fire protection was largely provided by uniformed black volunteers, and among them was Capt. Henry Shelton (right). Equipment had evolved somewhat, with hoses reeled on carts to draw water from wells.

A menacing 1921 fire prompted the quick formation of a more formal Rockville Volunteer Fire Department. With donations and some town funding, a state-of-the-art Ford Model T Waterous fire engine was purchased for $3,800 within a year; the volunteers proudly posed with the newly acquired vehicle in front of the Red Brick Courthouse. When an alarm sounded, men rushed to grab color-coded rings that determined who rode on the truck, while others followed in cars.

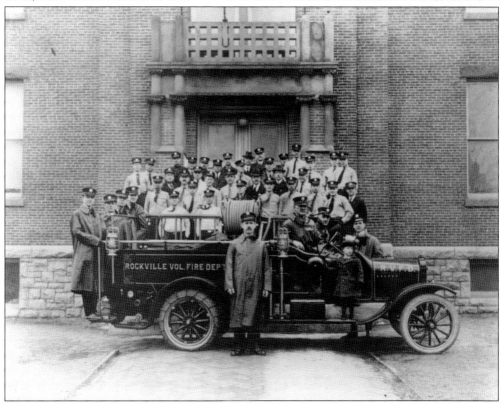

The county fairground—where Richard Montgomery High School now stands—dates to the mid-1800s. In 1846, Rockville farmers helped establish the Montgomery County Agricultural Society, which held the first county fair in Courthouse Square. A few years later, it gained a permanent location and became a weeklong annual attraction. By the early 1900s, the fair's most prominent feature was a grandstand and oval racetrack used first for horse racing and then car racing, which took over in popularity in the 1920s. Dr. Edward Stonestreet's office was moved to the fairgrounds to serve as a ticket booth. (Above, courtesy of Montgomery History; below, courtesy of Jeanne Gartner.)

Largely through the work of volunteers and a small collection of books initially housed in a law office, a library in Rockville came about shortly after the Civil War. Later homes included the former Stonestreet office from 1920 to 1936; it then used the vacant Rockville Academy. By 1939, the library, still run by volunteers, boasted about 5,000 volumes. Advocates for a public, countywide system made their case at the fairground in 1928. (Courtesy of the Library of Congress.)

Even after Montgomery County formed a library system, the Rockville Library continued operating independently for five years, joining the county system in 1957. It got its own branch building in 1971, was designated a regional library three years later, moved to anchor Rockville Town Square in 2006, and was later renamed Rockville Memorial Library to honor the county's fallen soldiers. The 1971 library (pictured) was razed for the Maryland District Court one week after being designated a Rockville historic district.

A big annual city tradition is the Memorial Day parade. This 1959 photograph shows a convoy of military jeeps coming up North Washington Street, past toy and shoe stores and a Woolworth's; beyond was the Rockville Center strip mall, built just a few years earlier.

Rockville has marked other important occasions with parades. Just six years after the one celebrating the construction of the 1939 post office, there was greater reason to celebrate with the nation's victory over Japan in World War II. Following the V-J Day parade, Mayor Douglas Blandford spoke from the Grey Courthouse steps. (Roy Perry collection.)

One of the buildings the Grey Courthouse replaced in 1931 was a Masonic lodge. Located on Montgomery Avenue at Washington Street (a prominent spot), it is pictured above sitting on large wooden planks for moving across Washington Street to the middle of the block; it alone among several buildings on the courthouse site was spared demolition. Despite being elegantly remodeled, it nonetheless met the same fate in 1973 and was replaced by an office building. Its demolition sparked the formation of Peerless Rockville a year later.

The Galilean Fishermen's Temple on Washington Street was built in 1912 by a black fraternal organization to serve as a gathering spot and to host social and cultural events for African Americans. The organization also provided services not otherwise accessible in a segregated society, such as burial insurance. It was razed in the 1960s for a gas station. The city's Memorial Day parade tradition grew out of the organization's annual Decoration Day festivities that began with a parade and ended with a picnic and ball games.

The Rockville 30 Club was another fraternal organization. Its band is seen posing in front of the temple in 1930. The band often led the Decoration Day parade.

The national pastime played out locally in notable ways, with such teams as the Rockville Athletics and Red Sox. The 1933 Rockville team (above) ended its season on top. For the African American community, baseball was more than a game; it strengthened bonds among communities near and far and served as a respite from restrictions within wider society. In 1920, the black Rockville team pictured below played at Griffith Stadium in Washington, DC. For a time, white and black teams played against each other once yearly.

These cars are definitely vintage, but not the photograph. Since 1961, the city has sponsored an annual antique car show at Civic Center Park, which draws hundreds of exhibitors and thousands of visitors. Seen here is the 53rd annual event in 2014. (Courtesy of City of Rockville.)

Members of the newly formed Rockville Chamber of Commerce enjoyed a 1927 swimming outing. Appearances can be deceiving; in customary attire, the organization, like many others, contributed greatly to the community through countless service projects.

Seven

A City of Neighborhoods

"Welcome to Our Neighborhoods," proclaims a sign on present-day Rockville's outskirts. The city is indeed a collection of distinct residential areas, nearly all created by developers over time, ever expanding the boundaries of Rockville outward in all directions and resulting in a sort of mosaic.

In the century since becoming the county seat, Rockville's growth had been gradual. But with the railroad's arrival, whole new neighborhoods came about—first east of the train station, including one for African Americans, and then a large speculative subdivision that became what is now the historic West End.

A far more explosive growth spurt occurred in the 20th century, the post–World War II building and population boom exponentially increasing Rockville in size through annexation of outlying new developments and truly transforming it into a city.

The most significant of these was Twinbrook, eclipsing established neighborhoods not only in size but impact. Its modest but expandable homes were quickly bought up by returning servicemen starting families. Before streets could be paved, 300 homes were occupied. Twinbrook Elementary, built in 1952 as baby boomers reached school age, was doubled in size just a year later; even so, Glenview Mansion, purchased for civic purposes, was temporarily pressed into service to house students.

The following decades brought "planned communities," as they were termed, to underscore the packaging of a range of neighborhood elements in a comprehensive design. From the varying mix of home types and amenities, like parks and commercial areas, have come neighborhoods each with a distinctiveness all their own.

Whatever their roots, many neighborhoods—Burgundy Knolls, Fallsmead, Glenora Hills, Montrose, Rockshire, and Silver Rock to name just a few—constitute Rockville, and the city government officially counts more than 100. Quite a mosaic!

ROCKVILLE PARK

Rockville, Montgomery Co., Maryland.

LOTS FOR SALE

$150.00

UNIFORM PRICE.

FIVE DOLLARS

CASH,

$5.00

PER MONTH

Without Interest.

Limited Number.

$150.00

IS THE PRICE!

CALL EARLY

Or You Will

Miss this Chance

LOCATION.

ROCKVILLE is located about sixteen miles out on the Metropolitan Branch of the Baltimore and Ohio Railroad. It has long been known only as the County Seat of Montgomery County; in more recent years it has become gratefully recognized by the citizens of Washington as one of the most delightful and healthy locations for summer residences. Its elevation, pure water, beautiful views, and charming society combined make this place a favorite resort for those Washingtonians who cannot spare the time or afford the expense of taking extended trips to the sea shore or mountains. Here the department clerk may own his cottage, have his own garden, raise fowls, or flowers, or any of his pet hobbies. With almost hourly communication with the city. One-half hour's ride puts him in the city, ready for business. Within one hour after leaving his desk he can be at home, with the long summer evening his own. His wife and children are far away from the dangerous and disagreeable heat of the city, breathing pure air, and enjoying the lovely country.

Rockville Park

Is *in* Rockville, right at the depot, yet considerably above the grade of the railroad. It covers the crest of the most elevated plateau in the neighborhood and commands extensive views on all sides. However, the lots are all level, with slopes of easy grade. Of course the corporation will eventually put down brick sidewalks, but at present have not funds to do so; as a substitute the owner of this tract will put down, at his own expense, a plank walk from the depot, extending in front of every lot in the subdivision. He also enters into a contract with the purchasers to set out a shade tree in front of each lot.

The proximity of the churches, schools, post-office, and depot makes this location one of the choicest parts of Rockville.

To secure a lot in this choice sub-division it will be necessary to act promptly, as the number is limited.

Price and Terms.

THE lots in Rockville Park are not all of uniform dimensions, but all contain about the same number of square feet, thus equalizing the differences in width and length. The price is the same for all—one hundred and fifty dollars ($150) apiece. Comparing the relative location of this tract with other lots in Rockville which have recently been sold, the price I ask is cheaper by 50 per cent. The lots referred to are over a mile from the depot, while Rockville Park is at the depot. Within six to eight squares of Rockville Park lots have recently sold for over one thousand dollars apiece, and are now being improved by the erection of handsome residences thereon.

The price of $150 per lot is within the reach of all, and offers a splendid opportunity for persons of small means to acquire property that is sure to grow more valuable each year, and to accommodate such persons I have made my terms as easy as possible, charging no interest on the deferred payments. I will sell these lots at the uniform price of $150 per lot, and require a cash payment of only $5, and $5 on or before the 5th day of each month, following the date of purchase, thus giving the purchaser two and one-half years to make all his payments. I will allow a discount of ten (10) per cent. for all cash or for all cash advances in sums of not less than twenty-five ($25) dollars on each lot.

Every lot is available for immediate improvement, and will make a pretty home. Several tasty houses have already been built on part of this tract.

Call early if you wish to buy and act promptly, as I cannot promise to reserve a lot for even a few hours.

Remember the terms, $5 cash and $5 per month; no interest. The price is absurdly low, and on such favorable terms that any one can buy. They are sure to bring more money in a very short time, and will probably double in value within a year or two. Such advantages cannot fail to be appreciated, and lots will be sought after by parties desiring to build.

Remember the price is only one hundred and fifty dollars, and only $5 cash on each lot required. Don't delay in making your cash payment, as this is absolutely necessary to secure a lot.

WASHINGTON DANENHOWER

1115 F Street N. W., WASHINGTON, D. C.

Rockville's first residential subdivision after the arrival of the B&O Railroad came in 1884 when a speculator bought 28 acres east of the train station. Naming it Readington after himself, he divided it into half-acre building lots but sold only six. DC developer Washington Danenhower bought the remainder in 1890, renamed the subdivision Rockville Park, reduced the lot sizes, and with ads like this was more successful. Thus, the East Rockville neighborhood was born.

PEERLESS ROCKVILLE

WHAT IT OFFERS TO
HOMESEEKERS AND INVESTORS.

Concurrent with the development of Rockville Park was the much larger 500-acre West End Park subdivision on the other side of town, the site of Julius West's farm. Another Washington developer, Henry Copp, offered quarter-acre lots on which purchasers built homes in the newest styles. To attract more buyers, he produced a 24-page booklet titled *Peerless Rockville* that proclaimed the town's "superiority [as] a place of residence" and showcased newly built homes in this montage.

RESIDENCES WITHIN WEST END PARK.

Handsome West End Park homes on expansive, manicured lots adorned postcards in the early 20th century (above); Rockville's historic West End of today retains most of them, making it a sought-after neighborhood. Every bit as desirable was a much smaller residential section at the other end of Rockville's main street, located on East Montgomery Avenue beyond the business district, as seen on the below postcard. As businesses encroached from downtown and the Rockville Pike, it declined; what was left of the neighborhood was razed along with the commercial section for urban renewal. (Above, courtesy of Montgomery History.)

MONTGOMERY AVENUE.   ROCKVILLE, MD.

Haiti (pronounced Hay-TIE) is Rockville's oldest-surviving African American neighborhood. Located along Martin's Lane just off North Washington, it was a pre–Civil War free black community augmented largely by slaves held by the Bealls and emancipated under Maryland's 1864 constitution or earlier. This drawing depicts a house built by Alfred Ross, one of those freed; it has remained in the family for generations. (Sketch by Colleen King.)

Created by merchant William Wallace Welsh about the same time as Copp's and Danenhower's subdivisions, Lincoln Park was an eight-acre subdivision northeast of the railroad station specifically for African Americans; most of the 50-some lots sold quickly. Through the 20th century, it became a tight-knit black community with marriages joining families. In 1959, Rockville built the first public housing project in the county, the 65-unit Lincoln Terrace, in Lincoln Park. This photograph was taken at the 1990 Lincoln Park Community Day, an annual event.

The Lincoln Park lots were quite narrow, evidenced by one of its most distinctive homes—the Cooke House on Lincoln Avenue, a standalone brick townhouse modeled on the family's previous residence in Pittsburgh. Most of the other first homes were modest wooden structures (at least two were log cabins), but some original landowners bought adjacent lots to build bigger homes, a few emulating the Victorians being built in the West End, though with less ornamentation. (RB photograph.)

Clarence "Pint" Israel, who grew up in Lincoln Park, played for several Negro League teams, including the Washington Grays and Newark Eagles. With the latter in 1946, he had a pinch-hit single off the legendary Satchel Paige in the Negro League World Series, helping his team clinch the title. After his career, he returned to live in Rockville; a recreational area next to Lincoln Park Community Center is named in his honor.

Two late 1930s to early 1940s developments—with already constructed houses offered for sale, not simply lots—presaged the coming post–World War II housing boom. This 1940 ad for Roxboro, just west of Chestnut Lodge, offered modest five- and six-room Cape Cod and ranch-style houses.

Rockcrest, south of Veirs Mill Road and east of First Street, offered similarly modest, mostly wooden homes. Assistance provided by the Federal Housing Administration created in the New Deal helped many buyers. Across Veirs Mill Road, Lone Oak Elementary, the first of a rash of new schools, opened in 1950 to accommodate the postwar baby boom. One student was Tom Curtis, six years old in this Christmas 1952 photograph, which provides a glimpse of the neighborhood.

The construction of Twinbrook (originally hyphenated as "Twin-Brook" for two Rock Creek tributaries) may have been as consequential in Rockville's evolution as the railroad's arrival. A quintessential large, rapidly built post–World War II development, it ultimately encompassed several hundred acres on both sides of Veirs Mill Road just west of Rock Creek. Developers, including Joseph Geeraert (pictured), built it in phases and pieces with names like Twinbrook Forest and Halpine Village. Some streets were named to commemorate the war, its battles, and generals. In 1955, seven years after the first residents moved in, the community raised funds for an Olympic-sized pool—some residents pitched in to dig out the spot by hand.

Twinbrook's compact but easily expandable houses could hardly be built fast enough. Veterans financed purchases almost entirely with GI loans. After the city annexed it and other earlier subdivisions to its east, Rockville's land area and population ballooned roughly tenfold between 1940 and 1960, going from 466 acres to 4,473 and from 2,047 residents to 26,090.

In the early 1950s, part of Dawson Farm became the Hungerford Towne subdivision, also offering expandable homes. Because the scale of Twinbrook so taxed the municipal water system, Hungerford—as the neighborhood is now known—was delayed until the new Potomac River pipeline was built. This early ad touted its location "just a few blocks from the modern shopping facilities of Metropolitan Rockville." In 1957, a black family moved in; a proposal to restrict the community pool to whites was defeated 95-5 by residents.

Hungerford Towne

CAPE CODS EXPANDABLE TO 2, 3 OR 4 BEDROOMS, 2 BATHS!
To reach Hungerford this weekend, drive straight out Wisconsin Ave. directly to the outskirts of Rockville, Hungerford Towne is on left side of road, just a few blocks from the modern shopping facilities of Metropolitan Rockville, and right next to new Rt. 240 that will take you downtown in 20 minutes.

Copyright 1954
W. Evans Buchanan

3-bedroom expandables, $13,630
2-bedroom expandables, $12,950.
4-bedroom homes, $14,135.

Nothing Down
to qualified vets: Just settlement

MONTHLY PAYMENTS FROM $65
plus taxes and insurance
30-YEAR LOANS
FHA TERMS AVAILABLE

FULL BASEMENTS AVAILABLE IN ALL STYLES
Buchanan-Gingery, Builders. OL. 9-8304. PO. 2-6126

NEW MARK COMMONS

The 1960s brought a new type of development—the planned community. One of the most innovative, New Mark Commons clustered contemporary townhomes and detached residences carefully into the natural landscape to create a "Twentieth Century Village." Ample open space and preservation of trees were innovative hallmarks of the 96-acre community; its focal point was a lake created from existing streams, as seen above in an original sales brochure, which also shows the community's logo—the stylized initials NMC. The community's appearance has changed little, as is evident from the photograph below. A planned shopping area never came about; the first residents decided against it. The entire development was listed in the National Register of Historic Places in 2017 on its 50th anniversary. (Below, Roy Perry collection.)

Advertised as "Montgomery County's first preplanned community" with ready access to Interstate 70-S (now Interstate 270) and "country club living" to boot, Woodley Gardens offered not just a range of housing options, including single-family homes (as depicted above in a promotional brochure), rental garden apartments, and townhomes, but also an abundance of amenities, such as a shopping area, school, parkland, and community center with a pool. House prices started at around $20,000, which was considerably higher than the more modest postwar developments.

On the heels of Woodley Gardens, and just up the road, came a similar development built behind Montgomery College. Although marketed as "Plymouth Village" to tout its colonial homes, the legal name used on city plat maps was College Gardens, and that took hold among residents. Streets were named for colleges, just as those in Woodley Gardens had flower names.

The sprawling 430-acre King Farm is a more recent mixed-use development of homes, offices, and commercial enterprises—even a hotel and retirement community. It sits on one of the area's last big farms. Owned by W. Lawson King for much of the 20th century, it once claimed to have the world's largest Holstein herd and was a major milk supplier for Thompson's Dairy, which delivered its products to homes throughout the Washington area into the late 1960s. The farmhouse and barns were retained as a city park. Work began on the large development in 1997.

King Farm's largest park is named for an early resident, Mattie Stepanek, who died before his 14th birthday of a muscular disorder. In his short life, he became a well-known peace advocate and author of seven best-selling inspirational and poetry books—all while using a wheelchair and ventilator. A goodwill ambassador for the Muscular Dystrophy Association, he appeared several times on Oprah Winfrey's show; the celebrity made a surprise visit to the park's 2008 dedication and unveiling of a life-size statue of Mattie and his faithful service dog. (Courtesy of Edward Tenney and Jeni Stepanek.)

Rockville's westward expansion continued in the early 2000s with construction of Fallsgrove, featuring a variety of housing, a large shopping center, and community center, as depicted in this preconstruction rendering. The city's newest neighborhood, it was built on the 254-acre Thomas Farm west of Interstate 270. With a greater proportion of townhomes than was typical of Rockville's developments in the 1960s, both Fallsgrove and King Farm were higher-density communities and thus contributed to another significant jump in Rockville's population. By 2010, just over 61,000 people called Rockville home, making it Maryland's third-largest incorporated city; Frederick had eclipsed Rockville to take second place.

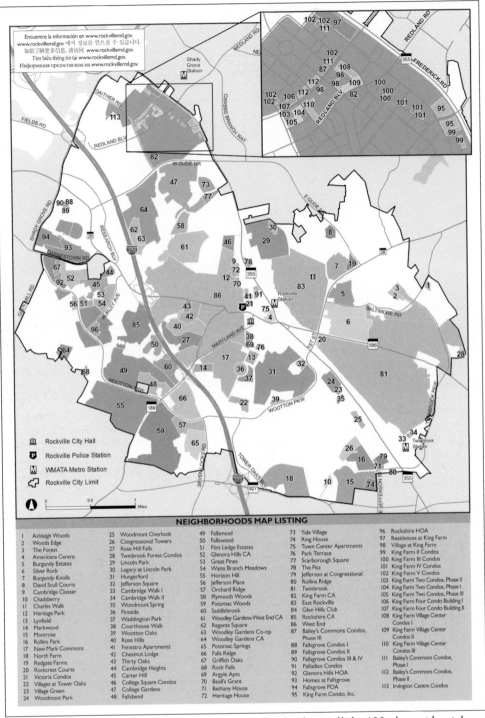

NEIGHBORHOODS MAP LISTING

1 Ashleigh Woods
2 Woods Edge
3 The Forest
4 Americana Centre
5 Silver Rock
6 Burgundy Knolls
7 Burgundy Knolls
8 David Scull Courts
9 Cambridge Cluster
10 Chadsberry
11 Charles Walk
12 Heritage Park
13 Lynfield
14 Markwood
15 Montrose
16 Rollins Park
17 New Mark Commons
18 North Farm
19 Redgate Farms
20 Rockcrest Courts
21 Victoria Condos
22 Villages at Tower Oaks
23 Village Green
24 Woodmont Park

25 Woodmont Overlook
26 Congressional Towers
27 Rose Hill Falls
28 Twinbrook Forest Condos
29 Lincoln Park
30 Legacy at Lincoln Park
31 Hungerford
32 Jefferson Square
33 Cambridge Walk I
34 Cambridge Walk II
35 Woodmont Spring
36 Fireside
37 Waddington Park
38 Courthouse Walk
39 Wootton Oaks
40 Rose Hills
41 Fenestra Apartments
42 Chestnut Lodge
43 Thirty Oaks
44 Cambridge Heights
45 Carter Hill
46 College Square Condos
47 College Gardens
48 Fallsbend

49 Fallsmead
50 Fallswood
51 Flint Ledge Estates
52 Glenora Hills CA
53 Great Pines
54 Watts Branch Meadows
55 Horizon Hill
56 Jefferson Place
57 Orchard Ridge
58 Plymouth Woods
59 Potomac Woods
60 Saddlebrook
61 Woodley Gardens-West End CA
62 Regents Square
63 Woodley Gardens Co-op
64 Woodley Gardens CA
65 Potomac Springs
66 Falls Ridge
67 Griffith Oaks
68 Rock Falls
69 Argyle Apts
70 Beall's Grant
71 Bethany House
72 Heritage House

73 Yale Village
74 Ring House
75 Town Center Apartments
76 Park Terrace
77 Scarborough Square
78 The Fitz
79 Jefferson at Congressional
80 Rollins Ridge
81 Twinbrook
82 King Farm CA
83 East Rockville
84 Glen Hills Club
85 Rockshire CA
86 West End
87 Bailey's Commons Condos, Phase III
88 Fallsgrove Condos I
89 Fallsgrove Condos II
90 Fallsgrove Condos III & IV
91 Palladian Condos
92 Glenora Hills HOA
93 Homes at Fallsgrove
94 Fallsgrove POA
95 King Farm Condo, Inc.

96 Rockshire HOA
97 Residences at King Farm
98 Village at King Farm
99 King Farm II Condos
100 King Farm III Condos
101 King Farm IV Condos
102 King Farm V Condos
103 King Farm Two Condos, Phase II
104 King Farm Two Condos, Phase I
105 King Farm Two Condos, Phase III
106 King Farm Four Condo Building I
107 King Farm Four Condo Building II
108 King Farm Village Center Condos I
109 King Farm Village Center Condos II
110 King Farm Village Center Condos III
111 Bailey's Commons Condos, Phase I
112 Bailey's Commons Condos, Phase II
113 Irvington Centre Condos

This 2017 map titled "Rockville: A City of Neighborhoods" shows all the 100-plus residential areas making up the city. It also shows its tremendous expansion from the tiny crossroads community—a relatively tiny area around the map's center designated by the police station. (Courtesy of City of Rockville.)

Eight

URBAN RENEWAL

By the 1960s, Rockville's historic downtown was languishing. Some stores in its business core had left for the Rockville Pike and elsewhere; many buildings were deteriorating. Officials embraced urban renewal to stem blight, spark commercial activity, separate pedestrians and traffic, and create a new identity for Rockville. Bold plans for a massive makeover emerged.

With a federal grant paying the bulk of the cost, the city demolished 100-some buildings over 46 acres north and east of the Red Brick Courthouse, which was also to be razed but was spared after public outcry. By 1972, most of the old business district was replaced by a stylish residential complex; a large indoor shopping mall with underground parking, designed by the noted architectural firm of Robert Geddes, Princeton University's dean of architecture, opened the same year.

While the residential Americana Centre proved successful, Rockville Mall struggled to attract shoppers and stores. Lacking national stores as anchors, it was never 100 percent occupied. By the early 1980s, more than half the retail space was empty, and the mall's bankrupt owners closed it. Various reincarnations and rescue plans agonizingly put together over the next decade proved equally unsuccessful.

Eventually, consensus formed around tearing the ill-fated structure down. Most of it was gone by 1995, and the city attempted to "start from scratch," as the *New York Times* noted.

Gradually, piece by piece—a pedestrian bridge to the Metro station, a new cinema, then apartment and office buildings, and finally, a large-scale mixed-use redevelopment project, all built on a restored grid of streets that had been eliminated—the city succeeded in producing a new bustling town center and the new identity hoped for a half-century earlier. Getting there closed a traumatic chapter in Rockville's history, and its old main street of varied buildings, some of historic and architectural merit that would be prized today, others clearly not, exists only in memory.

By the 1960s, when these two photographs were taken, many felt downtown Rockville had become obsolete, even shabby, and in need of revitalization. Previously well-patronized businesses on East Montgomery Avenue such as Roy's Place eatery and Steinberg's clothing store (above) were struggling. Many buildings, even ones across from the courthouses (below) that had been given new facades, appeared dated. Reformist city officials drafted a first-ever master plan and considered urban renewal options. (Below, Roy Perry collection.)

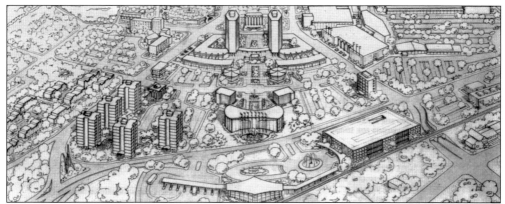

This rendering depicted a 1962 urban renewal plan presented to the public that envisioned a wholesale "new Rockville," one which "wipes out any hint of obsolescence," as *American City* magazine put it. The five high-rises on the left were an early vision of Americana Centre; above them near the top is the county office building—about all that would remain of old Rockville. Traffic would largely be directed around a large new pedestrian-friendly central city dominated by twin towers and a shopping mall (to the right).

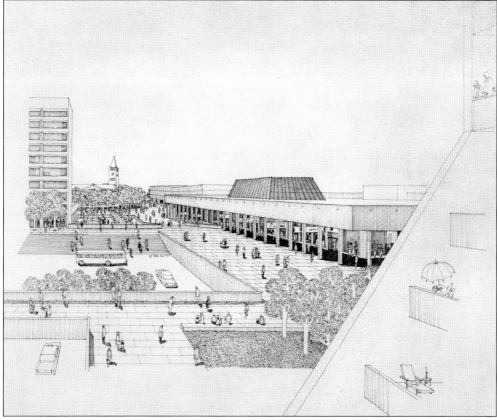

A relatively scaled-down project emerged, consisting of two main components, as this 1967 rendering shows: an indoor shopping mall flanked by high-rise residences. The lively scene conveys the hoped-for revitalization; unlike the earlier plan, this one preserved the Red Brick Courthouse, seen in the background.

To make way for "modern suburban living," as the sign above promised, much of old Rockville was leveled beginning in 1965. The 1970 panoramic shot below shows only the two courthouses still standing, along with a recent office building and the former Montgomery County National Bank (at far left). Even a small office building that replaced Vinson's Pharmacy a few years earlier was razed, the same fate awaiting the handsome old bank building. (Above, courtesy of Montgomery History; below, Roy Perry collection.)

Plowing over some of the remains of the bank building, this bulldozer then leveled the Brosius Building, an Art Deco structure that had once housed the post office and various businesses. Reflecting the decline of the city's center, its last use was as a pool hall. (Courtesy of Montgomery History.)

Americana Centre took the place of much of the East Montgomery Avenue business district and gave Rockville its first, now iconic, high-rise. This 1972 photograph shows the newly completed residential complex, a signature project of local builder Carl M. Freeman, juxtaposed with a few buildings awaiting demolition. Its mix of townhomes and high-rise and garden apartments proved popular and remains so. In 2018, it was designated a historic district of its own. (Roy Perry collection.)

The above 1971 view from Perry Street—now Maryland Avenue—shows Rockville Mall's steel framework nearly complete. When the mall opened the following year, the far section of this street along with the road in front of the courthouses was made a pedestrian plaza. The main entrance to the mall was situated on the plaza, as seen below. The mall abutted the building (on the left) that was one of the few spared for urban renewal (seen also from the rear on page 106). Now somewhat altered, it is 30 Courthouse Square; today's Maryland Avenue runs right through where the mall's entrance was. (Both, Roy Perry collection.)

Besides the pedestrian entrance, the other means of access to the mall was by car via a ramp off Hungerford Drive into an enclosed garage. Many motorists, however, found it dark and confusing; some felt unsafe.

The mall opened on Valentine's Day 1972 with events that generated excitement and attracted crowds, but shoppers' ranks thinned quickly. The large concrete structure came to be viewed as uninviting and even fortress-like. It was intended to have two big chain stores as anchors, but opened with DC-based Lansburgh's as the sole anchor; the store went bankrupt in under a year. As shoppers dwindled, vacancies proliferated. (Roy Perry collection.)

This 1972 aerial photograph shows the enormity of Rockville Mall; it occupied several blocks from Hungerford Drive at the top of the image to Farmers (now M&T) bank, the tall building at center right. The Americana Centre towers are at top right.

With the mall struggling early, various rescue efforts were undertaken. In 1974, the pedestrian entrance was dressed up with a modernist fountain to attract more foot traffic; even so, wrote one historian, "the plaza failed to fulfill its function as a gathering place and civic space." (Roy Perry collection.)

The mall was renamed in 1978 in another effort to boost its sagging fortunes, but tenancy dwindled further, and its owner declared bankruptcy in 1981. A new owner took a wrecking ball to a portion of the building in 1984, as seen above, reconfigured the remainder, and called it Rockville Metro Center to try to take advantage of the new Metro station. It still struggled, and the majority of the remaining mall was demolished in 1995—a portion survives, unrecognizable, as an office building at 255 Rockville Pike.

Where the mall had stood, new buildings, mostly offices and apartments, were erected over time, but the spark that succeeded in drawing people back downtown was the 1998 opening of a plush, multiscreen theater complex, now Regal Cinemas. A new town center was coming into being with a new millennium. (RB photograph.)

The biggest boost to Rockville's revival was a $370 million public/private project completed in 2007; the above photograph captured its 2004 ground breaking by developers and officials, including Gov. Robert Ehrlich (fifth from the left). Dubbed Rockville Town Square, it has succeeded in giving Rockville a thriving, lively new downtown area. The multi-block complex combined ground-level stores and restaurants, nearly 700 apartment and condo units above, surface parking and garages throughout, a large plaza with the library relocated there (left), and wide walkways connecting it all. (Left, courtesy of Simmons B. Buntin.)

Nine

NATIONAL AND NOTEWORTHY

Like most communities, Rockville has been shaped largely by local events and its residents. But there is another, less common dimension to Rockville's history: it has numerous ties to significant national events and noteworthy individuals. One such example has been noted previously—J.E.B. Stuart's time spent in Rockville proved costly, perhaps leading to a turning point in the Civil War.

Very much related to that war, a six-year-old child born into slavery was bought at auction, separated from his mother, and brought to Rockville. Fast forward—his autobiography, *The Life of Josiah Henson, Formerly a Slave, Now an Inhabitant of Canada*, inspired Harriet Beecher Stowe to write her enormously influential antebellum antislavery novel *Uncle Tom's Cabin*.

In the 20th century, one of the first legal challenges to segregated schooling occurred in Rockville with a lawsuit brought by civil rights icon Thurgood Marshall on behalf of a black Rockville teacher paid half what a similarly qualified white teacher earned. An icon of a different sort, celebrated Jazz Age novelist F. Scott Fitzgerald never lived in Rockville but lies at eternal rest near a busy downtown intersection; an annual festival in his honor has drawn a raft of equally renowned authors.

Also notable, a pioneering psychiatric treatment facility drew an eminent female clinician fleeing Nazi Germany; a patient who benefited from her innovative therapy wrote about it in the popular novel *I Never Promised You a Rose Garden*. A school bus–train collision prompted stronger railroad crossing safety measures nationwide, and Bob Woodward reported for the *Sentinel* just before joining the *Washington Post* soon after a break-in at the Watergate, and, well, the rest is history.

Rockville has been recognized as an All-America City four times, underscoring it as a locality with national stature. These local-national connections are yet another way Rockville has shown itself as, if not "peerless," definitely remarkable.

Josiah Henson's life was extraordinary. Born a slave, six-year-old Henson was sold and separated from his mother at a slave auction; he was bought by Rockville's Adam Robb and was enslaved on a nearby plantation for the next 30 years. Ultimately, he escaped to Canada and published his autobiography to raise money to free his brother, enslaved in Rockville by the Bealls. Harriet Beecher Stowe modeled the title character in *Uncle Tom's Cabin* on Henson; her 1852 novel is credited with galvanizing antislavery sentiment. In Canada, Henson established a thriving community for others fleeing slavery, gained fame as "Uncle Tom," was invited to the White House, and even met Queen Victoria in London, where this portrait was taken. He updated his autobiography several times; an 1881 edition included this depiction of his mother pleading—unsuccessfully—not to be separated from her son at the auction that brought him to Rockville. (Left, courtesy of the Smithsonian Institution; below, courtesy of Dorothy and John Foellmer.)

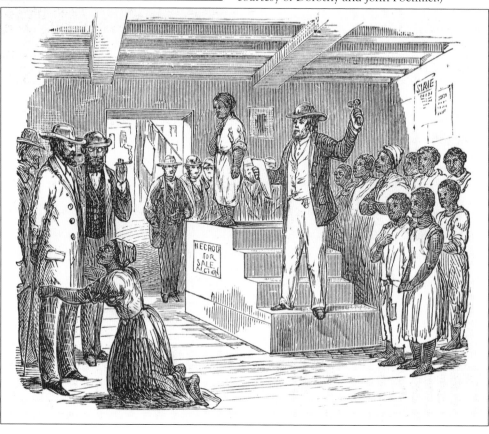

A young Thurgood Marshall (above, center) is seen outside the Grey Courthouse in 1937 when he came to Rockville to argue the first-ever lawsuit challenging unequal salaries for black public school teachers, brought by Rockville's William B. Gibbs Jr. Assisting him was the equally legendary Charles Hamilton Houston (left), who was Howard University law school dean when Marshall and Edward Lovett (right) earned their law degrees there several years earlier. Although largely ignored by area newspapers, the case garnered major coverage in the black press (below) and is regarded as an early milestone in Marshall's long legal pursuit to overturn school segregation, as the US Supreme Court ruled unanimously in a landmark 1954 decision. (Both, courtesy of *The Afro-American*.)

THE AFRO AMERICAN

A WASHINGTON NEWSPAPER FOR WASHINGTONIANS
CONTENTS OF THIS NEWSPAPER COPYRIGHT 1937 BY THE AFRO-AMERICAN CO.
TRADEMARK REGISTERED

45th Year, No. 41.   WASHINGTON, D. C., JUNE 12, 1937   Prices: 7c in D.C.; 10c Elsewhere

EQUAL PAY WAR OPENS

Washington Senators ace Walter Johnson—often called the greatest pitcher ever—gives tips to captivated youngsters at the athletic field behind the 1905 high school (seen in the background). Elected to the Baseball Hall of Fame in the original 1936 class, he won a different election as a Montgomery County commissioner two years later, bringing him to the county seat frequently. He is buried in Rockville Cemetery. (Courtesy of the Library of Congress.)

Lorenzo Dow Turner, known as the father of Gullah studies, grew up in Lincoln Park in the early 20th century. He earned a master's degree at Harvard and doctorate at Chicago and taught at Howard and Fisk Universities; his first academic appointment in South Carolina sparked an interest in the nearby Sea Islands residents' dialect. He traced their speech to African languages, launching a new field of linguistic study. His father, teacher Rooks Turner, came to Lincoln Park from North Carolina, where he started a black school but fled after a racial altercation. (Courtesy of the Smithsonian Institution.)

The nationally known private psychiatric hospital Chestnut Lodge operated from 1910 to 1999. Run by four generations of the founding Bullard family, it occupied the former Woodlawn Hotel. Standing next to an ambulance, head nurse Agnes Simpson is pictured in July 1930. Chestnut Lodge also encompassed medical, therapeutic, recreational, lodging, and other facilities over 88 acres in the West End. Joanne Greenberg's popular 1964 novel *I Never Promised You a Rose Garden* was based on her stay there. The main 1889 building was to be converted into condominiums when destroyed by fire in 2009.

Frieda Fromm-Reichmann, a prominent pioneering psychiatrist, came to Chestnut Lodge in 1935 to escape Nazi Germany; the facility's preeminence attracted her to it over others wooing her. Known for her innovative, highly individualized psychotherapeutic treatment methods, she spent the rest of her life at Chestnut Lodge, residing and seeing patients in a cottage on the grounds built especially for her; it is one of several historic properties maintained by Peerless Rockville.

From this small, plain structure in the backyard of his Rockville home, Edwin Smith, an official of the US Coast and Geodetic Survey, made some of the first astronomical measurements of the earth's "wobble" in the early 1890s. Through a subsequent international program created to understand the phenomenon better, six observatories were sited across the globe; Smith built one in nearby Gaithersburg, shown below in a 1910 photograph. The two halves of the roof slid apart, allowing a telescope to make observations. Used until 1982, the structure is a national historic landmark in its original location, now a Gaithersburg park. The other observatories were in Ohio, California, Japan, Russia, and Italy, roughly equidistant apart. (Below, courtesy of the National Park Service.)

Smith's observatory sat behind this 1890 Forest Avenue house he designed and built; descendants still live there. Smith's daughter Lucy resided there her entire life; she is showing the observatory to a visitor in the top photograph on the opposite page. She—and the house—had parts in the 1964 movie *Lilith*. She played the grandmother of Warren Beatty's character; a scene with both in the house appears at right. "Miss Lucy," as she was widely known, said her film career was "worth enough to repaper the house." The movie included other scenes around Rockville—even the Villa Theatre, which later screened the film, made an appearance. Beatty played a Chestnut Lodge worker infatuated with a patient, the title character.

A horrific 1935 train–school bus crash where Baltimore Road once crossed the railroad tracks killed 14 and injured 13 Williamsport, Maryland, students returning from a field trip late at night. Rockville residents helped at the scene and were still drawn to the site the next day, pictured above. (Note that the train station is visible on the right.) The back of the bus bore the brunt of the impact (below); surviving students were riding up front. In response to the accident, Pres. Franklin Roosevelt called for elimination of at-grade crossings nationwide and pledged federal financial assistance for bridge construction. Within two years, Rockville built the Veirs Mill Road bridge to carry traffic over the tracks. (Both, courtesy of Debra Carbaugh Robinson.)

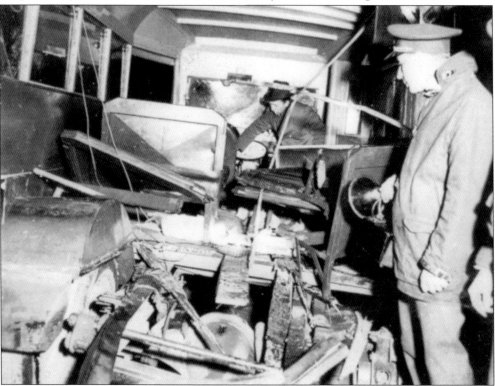

Rockville had connections to two important Watergate figures. Bob Woodward, half of the *Washington Post* duo that uncovered the scandal in 1972, worked the prior year at the *Sentinel* to gain more reporting experience after initially being rejected for a *Post* job. Watergate burglar—and Rockville resident—James McCord allegedly used this phone booth on Frederick Road near College Gardens Parkway to secretly communicate with the White House. Later, as he awaited sentencing at his home, he wrote to Judge John Sirica detailing perjury and political pressure—explosive charges that led to Senate hearings and, in turn, the unravelling of Richard Nixon's presidency. (Right, courtesy of Max van Balgooy; below, courtesy of the National Archives and Records Administration.)

JAMES W. McCORD, JR.
7 WINDER COURT
ROCKVILLE, MARYLAND 20850

FILED

MAR 23 1973

TO: JUDGE SIRICA   JAMES F. DAVEY, Clerk   March 19, 1973

Certain questions have been posed to me from your honor through the probation officer, dealing with details of the case, motivations, intent and mitigating circumstances.

In endeavoring to respond to these questions, I am whipsawed in a variety of

1. There was political pressure applied to the defendants to plead guilty and remain silent.

2. Perjury occurred during the trial in matters highly material to the very structure, orientation, and impact of the government's case, and to the motivation and intent of the defendants.

my 6th amendment right to counsel ~~and possibly other~~ and possibly other rights.

Famed author F. Scott Fitzgerald is buried in St. Mary's cemetery with his flamboyant wife, Zelda. Visitors frequently leave objects related to the Jazz Age novelist's life. Both were originally buried in Rockville Cemetery, but the couple's daughter—herself now buried adjacent to them—arranged for their reinternment in 1975 so her father could be with generations of his father's family, who farmed in Gaithersburg. (RB photograph.)

Since 1996, the centenary of Fitzgerald's birth, an annual literary festival named for him has honored acclaimed authors. The 2007 recipient of the Fitzgerald Award for Achievement in American Literature, Jane Smiley, is seen registering her delight. Other honorees include E.L. Doctorow, Richard Ford, William Kennedy, Norman Mailer, Alice McDermott, Joyce Carol Oates, Grace Paley, Annie Proulx, Richard Russo, William Styron, and John Updike, all of whom, like Smiley, are Pulitzer Prize winners.

Ten

TIME WAS . . .

History is measured in years; clocks keep track of much shorter time periods, of course, but nothing better symbolizes the passage of time than a clock—once called a timepiece, aptly enough.

A stately town clock once proudly stood in the center of Rockville, befitting its status as the heart of Montgomery County. A 1939 gift to the city, the clock unfortunately had an unexpectedly short life—less than two decades—but was promptly replaced. The replacement's life, while longer, was less stable, one might say, as it was moved from spot to spot with alterations to Rockville's downtown in the second half of the 20th century.

Removed in the late 1960s for the urban renewal project, it was in storage until placed in a small park near its original location to commemorate the nation's—and county's—bicentennial in 1976, then given new prominence next to the Rockville Mall entrance. But when the mall did not live up to expectations and was razed, the clock needed a new home.

Perhaps fittingly, that new home is on East Montgomery Avenue. Of course, not the road that was Rockville's main business street until urban renewal—that thoroughfare was eliminated—but a new, relocated East Montgomery Avenue. Albeit shorter, the namesake may be as significant to the "new" Rockville as the former thoroughfare once was, as the theater, constructed there along with some small shops and eateries in the late 1990s, began attracting people back downtown, precisely where the mall had once been, and the revival of Rockville followed.

So now, standing right in front of the theater, the clock keeps track of a promising forward march of time for Rockville.

The first town clock was given by the estate of a DC confectioner (why is not entirely clear), but the four-sided timepiece once stood in front of his first store at Twelfth and G Streets NW. This 1939 photograph shows it awaiting placement next to a statue of a Confederate soldier in a triangular park opposite the Red Brick Courthouse. The statue was itself a 1913 gift from the United Daughters of the Confederacy, who objected to the clock sharing the spot, so the latter was erected several hundred feet away on a grassy median in front of the Grey Courthouse, as seen on this volume's cover. The statue was moved next to the Red Brick Courthouse for urban renewal; like many such statues elsewhere, it became more controversial and was moved in 2017 to private land outside Rockville.

In 1957, a volunteer fireman rushing to a blaze in his car struck and toppled the clock, leaving it beyond repair. The sign at left is a historical marker about Rockville during the Civil War that now stands in front of the Red Brick Courthouse.

Many residents missed being conveniently reminded of the time when downtown, so a year after the original clock's demise, the city installed a replacement. Although it had only two faces instead of four, like the original, it had once stood in downtown DC—in fact, only a few blocks away from the first clock's original location, at Ninth and F Streets NW, in front of a jewelry store. (Courtesy of District of Columbia Public Library.)

With the construction of Rockville Mall and closing of the road in front of the courthouses, the clock eventually found a new home by the mall's pedestrian entrance. It is seen here in the 1980s after the mall had been renamed the Commons at Courthouse Square. As that change and other efforts to boost business failed and the mall was razed, the clock has come to rest about a block away, standing in front of the Regal Cinemas on the new, relocated East Montgomery Avenue.

BIBLIOGRAPHY

Cavicchi, Clare Lise. *Places from the Past: The Tradition of Gardez Bien in Montgomery County, Maryland*. Silver Spring, MD: Maryland–National Capital Park and Planning Commission, 2001.

Clarke, Nina H., and Lillian B. Brown. *History of the Black Public Schools of Montgomery County, Maryland, 1872–1961*. New York, NY: Vantage Press, 1978.

Department of Community Planning and Development Services. *Historic Buildings Catalog*. Rockville, MD: City of Rockville, 2011.

Duffin, Sharyn R. "Realizing a Dream: Providing Opportunity Through Education." Rockville, MD: Peerless Rockville, 2017.

Hill, Warrick S. *Before Us Lies the Timber: The Segregated High School of Montgomery County, Maryland, 1927–1960*. Silver Spring, MD: Bartleby Press, 2003.

Kelly, Clare Lise. *Montgomery Modern: Modern Architecture in Montgomery County, Maryland, 1930–1979*. Silver Spring, MD: Maryland–National Capital Park and Planning Commission, 2015.

Lachin, Teresa B. *Rockville's Recent Past*. Rockville, MD: Peerless Rockville Historic Preservation, Ltd., 2012.

MacMaster, Richard K., and Ray Eldon Hiebert. *A Grateful Remembrance: The Story of Montgomery County, Maryland, 1776–1976*. Rockville, MD: Montgomery County Government, 1976.

McGuckian, Eileen S. *Historical and Architectural Guide to the Rockville Pike*. Rockville, MD: Peerless Rockville Historic Preservation, Ltd., 1997.

————. *Rockville: Portrait of a City*. Franklin, TN: Hillsboro Press, 2001.

————. *The Sesquicentennial of Rockville: Local Government at 150 Years*. Rockville, MD: The Mayor and Council of Rockville, 2010.

————, and Lisa A. Greenhouse. *F. Scott Fitzgerald's Rockville: A Guide to Rockville, Maryland, in the 1920s*. Rockville, MD: Peerless Rockville Historic Preservation, Ltd., 1996.

"Take a Walking Tour and Explore Rockville." www.rockvillemd.gov/DocumentCenter/View/975.

"Take a Walking Tour of Rockville's African American Heritage." www.rockvillemd.gov/DocumentCenter/View/978.

Van Balgooy, Mary. *Women Who Dared: A Guide to the Places in Rockville where Women Dared to Challenge Expectations Both in Society and in Themselves*. Rockville, MD: Peerless Rockville Historic Preservation, Ltd., 2010.

ABOUT PEERLESS ROCKVILLE

Peerless Rockville Historic Preservation, Ltd., is a nonprofit, community-based organization founded in 1974 to preserve buildings, objects, and information important to Rockville's heritage. Headquartered in the historic Red Brick Courthouse, Peerless Rockville advances its goals through education, example, advocacy, and community involvement.

The organization has been successful in saving numerous landmarks and creatively restoring them for active use. These include the B&O Railroad Station, Montrose Schoolhouse, Dawson Farmhouse, Baptist Cemetery, Wire Hardware Store, and Frieda's Cottage at Chestnut Lodge. It has been recognized with awards from state and county organizations for its efforts.

Committed to a broad-based presentation of the city's history reflecting its heritage and modern development and diversity, Peerless Rockville collaborates closely with public agencies, residents, businesses, and other groups to advance historic preservation in all parts of the city.

Peerless Rockville offers a broad range of programs and activities for the public. These include lectures, illustrated presentations, hands-on workshops, walking tours, house tours, and publications on Rockville and Montgomery County history. The organization holds in trust thousands of documents, artifacts, and objects related to the development of Rockville as a community. It maintains a research library and community museum located in the Red Brick Courthouse and open five days a week. Through the research library, educational programs and events, exhibits, publications, and social media, Peerless Rockville serves and assists civic and community groups, students, residents, and businesses on a continuing and frequent basis. Become a member, supporter, or volunteer today at the website.

More information about the organization and Rockville's history is available at www.peerlessrockville.org.

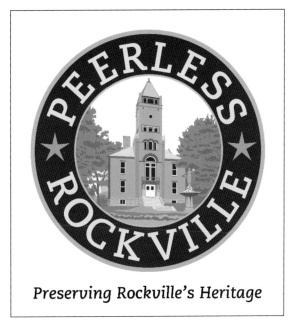

Preserving Rockville's Heritage

DISCOVER THOUSANDS OF LOCAL HISTORY BOOKS
FEATURING MILLIONS OF VINTAGE IMAGES

Arcadia Publishing, the leading local history publisher in the United States, is committed to making history accessible and meaningful through publishing books that celebrate and preserve the heritage of America's people and places.

Find more books like this at
www.arcadiapublishing.com

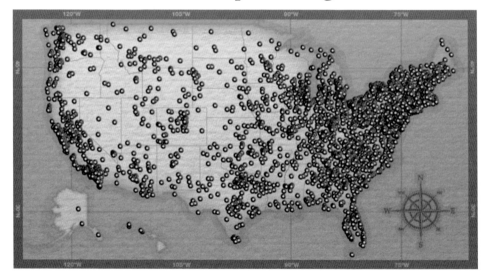

Search for your hometown history, your old stomping grounds, and even your favorite sports team.

Consistent with our mission to preserve history on a local level, this book was printed in South Carolina on American-made paper and manufactured entirely in the United States. Products carrying the accredited Forest Stewardship Council (FSC) label are printed on 100 percent FSC-certified paper.